LORRAINE PASCALE

Home Cooking Made Easy

LORRAINE PASCALE
Home Cooking Made Easy

100 fabulous,
easy to make recipes

Photographs by Myles New

HarperCollinsPublishers

HarperCollins*Publishers*
77–85 Fulham Palace Road,
Hammersmith, London W6 8JB

www.harpercollins.co.uk

First published by HarperCollins*Publishers* 2011

9 10

A catalogue record of this book is available from the British Library

ISBN 978-0-00-727592-2

Mixed Sources
Product group from well-managed forests and other controlled sources
FSC www.fsc.org Cert no. SW-COC-1806
© 1996 Forest Stewardship Council

FSC is a non-profit international organisation established to promote the responsible management of the world's forests. Products carrying the FSC label are independently certified to assure consumers that they come from forests that are managed to meet the social, economic and ecological needs of present and future generations.

Find out more about HarperCollins and the environment at
www.harpercollins.co.uk/green

Food styling: Annie Hudson
Props styling: Lisa Harrison

Printed and bound by Lego, Italy

The TV series was produced for BBC Television by Pacific Productions.

PACIFIC

Pacific
5–7 Anglers Lane, London NW5 3DG
T (+44) 207 691 2225
www.pacific.uk.com

Contents

Introduction

From scrumptious soups to sizzling lemon sole, cheeky cheesecakes and perfect peppermint creams, here are a hundred of my favourite recipes for relaxed home cooking.

I love nothing more than collecting recipes, testing them and sharing them with people – well, actually, I have to confess that eating the delicious results does give me a bit more pleasure…

Recently I've been like a mad food scientist in the kitchen; conducting culinary experiments using everyday ingredients and putting a wicked spin on some familiar traditional recipes. I've also drawn inspiration from my travels to Barcelona, Sri Lanka, Corsica and chilled-out Byron Bay, so be ready for a few surprises!

In this book are the kind of recipes that I like to cook on autumnal afternoons and cosy winter evenings. You'll find comfort in duvet day chicken noodle soup when the dark skies seem just a little too foreboding, and braised lamb shanks with Rioja and chorizo will bring the warmth and passion of an Iberian summer into the nippiest of seasons.

At one in the morning, standing in the kitchen covered in flour, I came up with another of the recipes that I've included here. While making a sugar syrup for toffee apples, I rifled through the cupboards and found some red food colouring. As I dropped a few beads of the scarlet liquor into the sugar syrup the mixture fizzled a bit. I swizzled it around in a heatproof glass jug and through the fog of a sugary fatigue I started drizzling crazy shapes on a sheet of baking parchment. When I lifted the band of now warm and hardening sugar and wrapped it around a freshly iced sponge cake sitting forlornly in a corner of the kitchen, graffiti cake was born!

For me, cooking can provide pure escapism into an aromatic realm of flavours, zests, glazes and textures. Sometimes this inspires me to reinvent recipes drawn from childhood memories, such as my sausage roll's big night out, which reminds me of the salami sticks my mum used to put in my school lunchbox.

It's important to me that I use ingredients that don't require a trip to an exotic foods store, and to include recipes that even the most inexperienced or reluctant cook can have a go at. Both my busy thirtysomething sister and my retired seventy-year-old dad have successfully cooked some of the recipes in this book.

I hope that there's something for everybody here. Whether you like an old-fashioned English muffin spread with lashings of butter, a not-so-Cornish pasty to take on those long winter walks, an oat couture granola bar for a quick-grab anytime snack, or the wonderfully retro and revamped caramelised pineapple and rum upside down cake to finish off the day.

In this book you'll also find recipes for homebaked breads, cakes, cookies, muffins and bars; soups, starters and canapés when you feel like making that extra effort and easy main meals for lunch or dinner that can cook slow or be rustled up super fast. If you're vegetarian or fancy a meat-free day, there are also some ideas for new slants on serving up your favourite veg. Not forgetting the sweet stuff; desserts such as my steamed chocolate pudding with warm Mars bar sauce that I could eat all by myself in one sitting, and a few of my favourite little extras – chutneys, sweets and other fine stuff.

Cooking at home, whether for family and friends or just for yourself, is one of life's great pleasures, and hopefully with these recipes I can show you that it can be relaxed and easy, too.

Starters, Soups, Canapés & Snacks

It's not every day that I serve starters and canapés, but when I do it's usually something quick, easy and super tasty. Bacon and mature Cheddar twisties have become a firm favourite in my house, so much so that I often make a large batch and store them in a plastic container for people to grab on the go. Needless to say, they don't usually last very long. My sausage rolls have a special twist, and the herbed Scotch eggs have a special place in my heart! On those I-don't-feel-like-going outside days, my duvet day chicken noodle soup gives edible relief, while roasted butternut squash soup with chilli and ginger is real food for the soul.

'One cannot think well, love well and sleep well, if one has not dined well.'

Virginia Woolf

Bacon & mature Cheddar cheese twisties

When I made a batch of these they were gone before they were even cool! These are in my top ten all-time favourite foods and are fantastically easy to make. For a little extra spice, sprinkle on some paprika or cayenne. Makes 14 twisties

1 x 375g puff pastry

Plain flour, for dusting

1 tbsp English mustard

100g mature Cheddar cheese, grated

Freshly ground black pepper

14 or so slices of really good-quality thin bacon (sadly, the regular stuff is just too salty) or 14 slices of prosciutto or pancetta

1 egg, lightly beaten, for the eggwash

Line a large baking tray with baking parchment and set aside.

Roll out the pastry on a lightly floured work surface to a large rectangle that is as long (when I say 'long' I mean the height from top to bottom) as one of the slices of bacon and as wide as you can roll it. The pastry should be about 5mm thick. Turn the pastry so that the longest side is facing you and spread the mustard over, then sprinkle with the cheese and black pepper. Lay the pieces of bacon down side by side as if they were all lying in bed together, leaving a 2mm gap between each piece. Then use a sharp knife to cut between each piece. Pick up one piece and twist it about 4–5 times so it looks like a curly straw, then put it on the prepared baking tray and repeat with the rest of the twisties, arranging them spaced apart, as they will spread a little during baking.

Put the trays in the fridge for 15–20 minutes to firm up, or in the freezer for 10 minutes. Preheat the oven to 220°C (425°F), Gas Mark 7. Remove the twisties from the fridge and brush the pastry with the eggwash. Put the baking trays into the oven, turn the oven down to 200°C (400°F), Gas Mark 6 and cook for about 20 minutes, or until the pastry is well risen and looks golden brown. Preheating the oven at a higher temperature compensates for any lost hot air when the oven is opened to put the twisties in. Otherwise, the oven temperature may drop to 180°C (350°F), Gas Mark 4 and it would not be hot enough to give the twisties that big blast of heat they need.

When they are cooked, remove them from the oven and leave to cool.

Sausage roll's big night out

I don't have people over for dinner too much these days, as there do not seem to be enough hours in the day. The few times a year I do, however, these sausage rolls make a regular appearance. I know salami sticks are not everyone's cup of tea, but all tucked up in puff pastry then lightly cooked they remind me of my youth, when Mum would put one in my lunch box along with egg-and-salad-cream sandwiches, prawn cocktail crisps and a carton of my favourite blackcurrant cordial. Makes 6

1 x 375g packet of puff pastry

Flour, for dusting

6 skinny regular-sized salami sticks, cut in half

1 egg, lightly beaten, for the eggwash

Preheat the oven to 220°C (425°F), Gas Mark 7. Cut the pastry in half and roll one half out on a lightly floured surface to a rectangle about 42cm wide and 9cm high (or the height of half the salami stick). Trim the edges with a sharp knife to neaten them a little if necessary. Lay a salami stick half on the pastry about 1cm from the left-hand side edge, then take another one and lay it 4cm away from that one. Repeat until you have four sticks lying side by side (but spaced apart on the pastry). This will use up half of your 42cm piece of pastry. Brush the side with the salami sticks with the beaten egg, brushing it well in between the gaps and all around. Fold the other half of the pastry over the sticks like a neat book and press down in between them so they are nicely covered and the pastry is fitted all around. The salami sticks may roll round a little, but gentle prodding will get them to their right place in the end. They should look like they have been tucked up in bed!

Now place this in the fridge to firm up, then repeat with the other half of the pastry and the remaining salami.

Once the pastry is firm enough, remove from the fridge and put one block on a chopping board. Place the pastry so that the salami sticks are horizontal like the rungs of a ladder. Using a sharp knife, cut a slice vertically about 1cm thick. Repeat all the way along with both blocks of pastry, then place each slice onto a baking sheet, spacing them about 2cm apart because they tend to spread during baking. Brush the pastry (try to avoid the salami sticks) with the eggwash and place in the oven. Turn the oven down to 200°C (400°F), Gas Mark 6 and cook for about 20 minutes, or until the pastry is well risen and golden brown. Have a peek through the glass at 15 minutes to see how they are doing, just in case they have cooked more quickly.

Goat's cheese truffles

Really cute and tasty little balls of yumminess. Makes 18–20

300g rindless goat's cheese log, fridge cold

Sea salt and freshly ground black pepper

Few squidges of honey

Suggested coatings

(Each amount coats about 2 balls)

2 tsp crushed pink peppercorns

1 tsp sesame seeds

½ tsp paprika

1 tbsp finely grated Parmesan cheese

1 tbsp finely chopped fresh chives

1 tbsp toasted and finely chopped hazelnuts

Prepare your chosen coating ingredients and put each one in a separate small bowl or ramekin. Choose a good combination of colours, flavours and textures.

Put the goat's cheese in a bowl and season, blending the salt and pepper in well. Break the cheese into bite-sized pieces, each about 15g (1 teaspoon) each and roll them into smooth balls measuring about 2.5cm in diameter.

Mix the honey with a few drops of water to loosen it a little and brush it all over a truffle. Place the ball in one of the coatings and swirl it around until it is evenly coated. Arrange on a serving platter and repeat until all the balls are coated.

Either eat at once or cover and refrigerate until almost ready to serve. The beauty of these is that they can be made ahead of time and then taken out of the fridge half an hour or so before guests arrive.

Roasted butternut squash soup with chilli & ginger

This is the soup that broke me – it turned me from being a model into wanting to be a chef. I made it one autumnal day in Battersea and the sweet, deep, slightly spicy taste blew me away. Makes about 1.2 litres, serves 4

1 medium butternut squash, about 800g, unpeeled, deseeded and cut in half from top to bottom

1 clove of garlic, unpeeled and squashed

2 tbsp olive oil

Sea salt and freshly ground black pepper

50g butter

1 large onion, peeled and finely diced

1 x 2cm piece of fresh ginger, peeled and finely grated

Pinch of dried chilli flakes (optional) or 1–2 chillies, deseeded and finely chopped (I like my chillies quite hot), plus extra to serve

900ml of liquid chicken stock (veggie stock is good but chicken stock usually has a better flavour)

Squeeze of lime juice

To serve

Splash of coconut milk

Few fresh coriander leaves

Preheat the oven to 220°C (425°F), Gas Mark 7. Put the butternut squash halves on a large roasting tray with the garlic. Slash the squash with a knife, then drizzle with a tablespoon of olive oil and season well. Roast in the oven for about 30–35 minutes, or until a knife inserted into the squash slides through easily and it is nice and soft.

While the squash is roasting, put the remaining tablespoon of oil and the butter in a large pan over a low heat. Add the onion and seasoning and leave to soften right down, stirring occasionally. This is a little time-consuming and can take up to 20 minutes or so, but it is worth it for the sweetness of flavour.

Remove the roasted squash from the oven and leave to cool a little, turn the oven off and pop some bowls in to warm. As soon as the squash is cool enough to handle, scoop the flesh from the skin and set aside, discarding the skin.

Once the onion is soft, squeeze in the roasted garlic clove, discarding the skin, then add the squash, ginger, chilli and stock. Bring to the boil then take it off the heat.

Next, get another large pan at the ready. Working in batches, blitz the soup in a blender, pouring the smooth soup into the clean pan. I like to blitz it until it is really, really smooth. Once all the soup has been blitzed, return the soup to the hob to heat through until piping hot. Taste and season with salt and pepper if you think it needs it. At this stage I often add a squeeze of lime juice, which really lifts the flavours of the soup.

Ladle the piping hot soup into the warmed serving bowls and serve with a little coconut milk drizzled over the top and a sprinkling of coriander leaves and finely sliced chilli.

Herbed baked Scotch eggs

I have a penchant for Scotch eggs. I buy them at the petrol station in the middle of long car journeys – I just fill the car up with petrol, then go into the shop and grab a Scotch egg and a packet of prawn cocktail crisps. However, when I have time, I like to make my own, and I use different types of sausagemeat to give them something a bit extra. Dipped in some mayonnaise or a large blob of salad cream, they really make my day. Makes 4

- Oil, for oiling and drizzling (you can use light oil spray if you like)
- 4 medium eggs
- 1 egg, lightly beaten
- 75g natural or golden dried breadcrumbs
- Small handful of fresh thyme leaves
- Pinch of ground nutmeg (optional)
- Salt and freshly ground black pepper
- Plain flour, for dusting
- Pinch of mustard powder
- 6 good-quality sausages, with their 'skins' removed

Preheat the oven to 200°C (400°F), Gas Mark 6 and line a baking tray with oiled foil. Put the whole eggs in a pan, cover with cold water and bring to the boil. Once the water is boiling, turn it down to a robust simmer and cook for 5 minutes. When the eggs are ready, remove the pan from the heat, take it to the sink and run cold water over the eggs for a minute or two to stop them cooking. Peel the eggs and set aside.

Put the lightly beaten egg in one bowl and the dried breadcrumbs, thyme and nutmeg along with a bit of salt and pepper in another bowl. Season the flour with salt and pepper and the mustard powder.

Put some clingfilm on the work surface, take 1½ sausages and squidge the meat down on the clingfilm. Squish it until is becomes a roundish flat circle, then take one egg and dip it into the seasoned flour. Put the egg in the middle of the sausagemeat and draw up the clingfilm around it so you have a little 'sac'. This is a great way of covering the egg with the sausagemeat and I find it beats trying to do it without. Now carefully peel away the clingfilm, leaving the sausagemeat around the egg. You may need to squish it down and around slightly on the egg if there are any gaps.

Now dip the meat-coated egg into the lightly beaten egg, making sure it is covered all over, then dip it into the breadcrumbs, rolling it around and pressing to secure any bits that are not sticking properly. Place the Scotch egg on the prepared baking tray and repeat with the other three eggs. Spray or drizzle a little oil over the eggs, then cook in the oven for about 20–30 minutes, or until the sausagemeat is cooked and the Scotch egg looks golden brown. Drain on kitchen paper.

These are lovely to take to work, or just to have in the fridge as a treat.

Caramelised spiced nuts

I like to make a big jar of these spiced nuts and pop them on the shelf to grab on the go when I fancy a naughty tasty snack. Makes about 600g

300g granulated sugar

450g mixed nuts, like cashews, pecans, hazelnuts, almonds, walnuts

1 tbsp sea salt

1 tsp paprika, plus extra to taste if necessary

1 tsp ground cinnamon, plus extra to taste if necessary

1 tsp ground cumin, plus extra to taste if necessary

300ml water

Preheat the oven to 180°C (350°F), Gas Mark 4 and line a large baking tray with parchment paper or use a non-stick baking sheet.

Put the sugar, nuts, salt and spices in a medium pan with the water and bring slowly to the boil, stirring until the sugar dissolves. Reduce the heat a little and simmer the mixture rapidly for about 15–20 minutes until the bubbles become thick and syrupy.

Strain the mixture through a colander set over a bowl (use oven gloves when handling the pan, as hot sugar can spit and splutter and burn you), then tip the nuts onto the prepared baking tray and spread them out in a single layer. Bake the nuts in the oven for 20 minutes, or until toasted.

Remove from the oven, leave to cool and harden before breaking the nuts into small pieces. Sprinkle with more spices if required. Store in an airtight container for a few days if not eaten straightaway.

Any leftover syrup is delicious drizzled over ice cream or on a poached pear.

Duvet day chicken noodle soup

Supreme comfort eating and good for the soul, too! The essence of a very good soup is a really good stock, jam-packed full of flavour. Homemade is best, but a decent liquid chicken stock bought from the shop works well too. Serves 4–6

- 1.5 litres good-quality chicken stock
- 1 bunch of spring onions, trimmed, sliced and separated into white bits and green bits
- 3 cloves of garlic, peeled and thinly sliced
- 1 red chilli, deseeded and finely chopped
- 1 x 2cm piece of fresh ginger, peeled and sliced into matchsticks
- 1 cinnamon stick
- 2 star anise
- 6 black peppercorns
- Sea salt flakes
- 3 skinless, boneless chicken breasts
- 1 stick of celery, trimmed and sliced into thin matchsticks
- 1 carrot, peeled and sliced into matchsticks
- 150g quick-cook thin noodles
- Small bunch of fresh basil leaves
- Small bunch of fresh mint leaves
- 1 lime, cut in half

Put the chicken stock into a large pan with the spring onion whites, garlic, chilli, ginger, cinnamon, star anise, peppercorns and a good amount of salt. Bring to a simmer, then carefully slide the chicken breasts in and cover with a lid. Cook for 12 minutes, then throw in the celery and carrot and cook for a further 5 minutes. Taste the soup and season as necessary.

Remove the chicken, cinnamon stick and star anise from the soup with a slotted spoon and at the same time put the noodles into the broth and cook, uncovered, for as long as needed.

While the noodles are cooking, flake the chicken into bite-sized pieces with two forks. Just before the noodles are ready, put the chicken back into the broth to heat through and taste the soup again to check if you need any more seasoning.

Rip up half of the basil and mint leaves, stir through the soup with the spring onion greens and then divide the soup among 4–6 bowls. Scatter the remaining herbs over the top and squeeze a little lime juice over each one to finish.

Pea soup with minted mascarpone

There is always a bag of peas or petit pois in my freezer. Peas are my vegetable of choice and I serve them most days of the week. The other thing I always have in abundance is mint. If you have ever tried to grow it, you will know the ease with which it slowly takes over the garden, winding its way through and over everything else in its path. The supply manages to keep up with demand; we are a mint-loving family and use mint in salads, teas, the odd alcoholic beverage and, of course, in soups. Serve this soup hot with a big chunk of fresh bread slathered with butter.

Makes 1.5 litres, serves 6

800ml chicken or vegetable stock

1kg frozen petit pois

Sea salt and freshly ground black pepper

A small handful of fresh mint leaves, finely chopped

4 dollops of mascarpone (about 150g)

Bring the stock to the boil in a large pan and add the peas. Cover with a lid and allow it to return to the boil. I always put a lid on while waiting for it to boil, as it speeds up the process quite considerably. Reduce the heat and simmer for 3 minutes, or until the peas are tender, then remove the pan from the heat.

Working in batches, blitz the peas and stock in a blender until smooth. Pour each batch into a clean pan as you go. Taste the soup and season with salt and pepper, then reheat it gently over a low heat.

Meanwhile, stir the mint through the mascarpone until well blended.

Once the soup has been heated through, divide it among serving bowls, put a dollop of the minted mascarpone on each one and serve piping hot.

Hot & spicy Bloody Mary soup

The morning after the night before in a steaming hot bowl of soup. Of course, the Vodka at the end is entirely optional but it does add a nice alcoholic kick, should the mood take you! I am not normally a fan of tomato soup, but this one is really full of flavour and will be one to remember. Makes about 1.2 litres, serves 4–6

- 1 tbsp olive oil
- 1 large red onion, peeled and sliced
- 500g ripe tomatoes (about 5 vine or plum tomatoes), roughly chopped
- 1 litre tomato juice
- 3 squirts of tomato purée
- 1 bay leaf
- 2 tbsp soft light brown sugar
- 50ml Worcestershire sauce
- ½–1 tsp cayenne pepper (depending how spicy you like it!)
- Sea salt and freshly ground black pepper
- Several shakes of Tabasco sauce (optional)
- Vodka, to taste (optional)
- 1 stick of celery, trimmed and cut into batons

Heat the oil in a large pan, add the onion and cook over a low heat for about 15 minutes until soft but not coloured. Add the tomatoes, tomato juice and purée, bay leaf, sugar, Worcestershire sauce and finally the cayenne and salt and pepper to taste. Bring to the boil, then reduce the heat a little to let it bubble away for a good 30 minutes to really get the flavours going.

Taste the soup and add more seasoning if needed, so it is just as you like it. Remove the bay leaf and discard. Then, working in two or three batches, ladle the soup into a blender and blitz until it is quite smooth but still has a little texture. Pour the blended soup into a large bowl or jug as you go. Once done, return it all to the pan and heat through gently. Add the Tabasco and Vodka, if using, and taste again, adjusting the seasoning if necessary.

Ladle the soup into warmed mugs or serving bowls and serve with the celery batons.

Deep-fried Camembert with a cranberry, Burgundy & thyme sauce

This dish is so naughty – in every way. It comes in the canapé chapter, but it is mightily fine as a meal in itself, to be perfectly honest. For me, life is too short to make cranberry sauce from scratch every time (except at Christmas!), so I like to buy a jar of ready-made and give it a little help from some herby friends. Serves 4

4 tbsp red wine, preferably Burgundy

Pinch of fresh thyme leaves

150g cranberry sauce

1 egg, lightly beaten

80g natural or golden breadcrumbs

Salt and freshly ground black pepper

1 x 250g whole Camembert, unwrapped

Vegetable oil, for deep-frying

Put the red wine in a small pan and boil it until it is reduced by half, this usually happens quite quickly. Add the thyme leaves and cranberry sauce, bring it to just below the boil, then take the pan off the heat and set aside.

Put the egg in one bowl and the breadcrumbs in another, then season the breadcrumbs with salt and pepper. Cut the Camembert into four pieces, then dip into the egg and then into the breadcrumbs. Dip once again into the egg and then into the breadcrumbs. Have a slotted spoon and tongs at the ready along with a wire rack with some kitchen paper underneath it.

Fill a medium, deep pan with oil to the depth of 6cm and heat over a medium heat until a small piece of bread carefully placed in the oil browns in 60 seconds.

Carefully place the breaded cheese into the hot oil, one by one, using a slotted spoon. Put them into the pan from a low height so that the hot fat does not splash, then deep-fry until they are a lovely golden brown colour. Remove the cheese with a slotted spoon or tongs – whichever is easier for you – and place them on the wire rack. Putting them on the rack rather than straight onto kitchen paper means that they will not be sitting in their own fat and will stay nice and crispy.

Once you have cooked all of the cheese wedges, place them on serving plates with the cranberry sauce and serve straightaway with a green salad.

Light & crispy tempura prawns & soy chilli dipping sauce

This is a great dish to impress friends. Prawns are perfect, but you could also use courgettes, aubergines, peppers and all sorts of vegetables as well if you like. I have made my own dipping sauce to serve with the tempura, but it is also delicious served with some ready-made chilli sauce. Serves 3–4

500ml vegetable oil, for deep-frying

100g plain flour

100g cornflour

Pinch of salt

2 tbsp baking powder

180–200ml very cold sparkling water

Few ice cubes (not essential but it helps)

10 large raw prawns, peeled with tails still intact

Dipping sauce

20ml soy sauce

20ml mirin

½ chilli, deseeded and finely diced

½ clove of garlic, peeled and finely diced

1 x 5mm piece of fresh ginger, peeled and finely diced (or to taste)

Lay some kitchen paper on the work surface and place a wire rack over it. I put deep-fried food on this as soon as it is cooked because the fat can drip down onto the kitchen paper through the rack; this is better than letting the food sit in its own oil if put directly on kitchen paper. Have a slotted spoon or tongs at the ready, whichever is easiest for you to use.

Fill a medium, deep pan with enough oil to reach 5cm depth (I used about 500ml) and heat over a medium heat until a small piece of bread carefully placed in the oil browns in 50–60 seconds.

Just as the oil is almost at the right temperature, put the flour, cornflour, salt and baking powder in a bowl. Make a well in the centre and add the water. Mix everything together very quickly until just combined. The batter should be quite thick and it does not matter if there are still lumps. Add 2 or 3 ice cubes, then dip one of the prawns in the batter and let the excess drip off until you can still see a bit of prawn through the batter. Carefully add the prawns to the hot oil from a low height so the fat does not splatter. Do not overcrowd the pan, as this lowers the temperature of the oil and makes the prawns boil rather than fry, so add them in small batches and deep-fry for 2 minutes. The prawns will cook in 2–4 minutes (although this depends on how big the prawns are). Tempura batter is very pale, unlike fish and chip batter, so when it starts going from white to pale golden, the prawns should be ready. Check one by cutting it open to see if it is cooked. It should be white and not too glassy looking, and you will now know how long to cook the other prawns.

Remove the prawn with a slotted spoon or tongs and place it on the wire rack to drain, then repeat with the others. There will be enough batter here for some vegetables too, which are delicious.

Combine the sauce ingredients in a bowl and serve with the hot prawns.

Prosciutto & Brie toastie

I used to go round to my friend's house in Witney for tea. Every so often, when cheese triangle sandwiches on white bread were not on the menu, her mum would fire up a machine that made the most perfect toasted cheese and ham sandwiches. I can never beat the perfection of those little triangle sandwiches, but this comes oh so close! Serves 2

- 6 slices of prosciutto (streaky bacon will work well too)
- Large knob of butter
- 4 slices of good thick crusty bread
- Oil, for frying
- 100–150g Brie, ripped up into chunks

Preheat the oven to 200°C (400°F), Gas Mark 6. Fry the prosciutto or bacon to just the way you like it, then set aside. Tip off any excess fat from the pan. Butter each slice of bread.

Heat some oil in a pan. Once the oil is hot, add two slices of bread, buttered side down, and divide the Brie and prosciutto or bacon between the bread. Put the other slices of bread on top, buttered side up, and using a fish slice, squish it down in the pan so it cooks more quickly. As soon as the bottom is toasty and golden brown, turn it over and cook the other side, squishing with the fish slice. I usually cook mine for about 2 minutes on each side. Once the toasties are cooked, remove them from the pan.

The chilli jam on page 229 goes well with this, but a big blob of brown sauce is also a match made in heaven!

Satay chilli chicken

A quick easy canapé or starter, or just a tasty snack. Serves 4

4 chicken breasts

Oil, for cooking

1 squidge of runny honey

1 small bunch of coriander leaves

Peanut sauce

100g crunchy peanut butter

1 clove of garlic, peeled and finely chopped

1 tbsp sesame oil

1–2 red chillies, finely chopped (depending on how hot you want it)

Pinch of soft light brown sugar

1 tbsp soy sauce

Juice of ½ lime

3–4 tbsp rice wine vinegar or mirin

1–2 tbsp water

Equipment

12 wooden kebab sticks cut so they can fit inside your biggest frying pan. Soak them in cold water for 30 minutes before using to prevent burning

Take a chicken breast and, using a pair of scissors and with the pointy end furthest away from you, cut the breasts into about three long thin strips, then set aside and continue with the other three chicken breasts.

Push a kebab stick along the length of a chicken piece, stopping just before the stick comes out the other end. Repeat with the rest of the chicken. Of course, if you don't feel like threading pieces of chicken on sticks, you can just skip this step and serve them as strips instead.

Heat some oil in a large sauté pan or frying pan, add the chicken and cook well on each side until the chicken is completely cooked. Depending on the thickness of the breast pieces, this will take about 8 minutes. My pan is not big enough to do all the chicken in one go, so I usually put about 1½ breasts' worth in at a time, then set them aside to cook the rest.

While the chicken is cooking, put all of the sauce ingredients into a blender and blitz to a rough consistency. Taste the sauce to see if you need to add any seasoning or perhaps a squeeze more lime juice, then set aside.

Once the chicken is almost cooked through, add a little honey to the pan and mix the chicken around in it until coated, then remove from the pan. If cooking the chicken in batches, leave the pan to cool a little, then wipe or rinse out the honey before adding the next batch, as it will burn if left in the pan. Add a little more oil and repeat with each batch.

Serve three satay sticks per person sprinkled with some coriander leaves and accompanied by the peanut sauce.

Breads

I have tried to make it my goal these days to bake a fresh hand-made loaf at least once a week. It is hard to beat the smell that meanders around the house as bread bakes in the oven. The first bread I ever made was at secondary school during my much loved Home Economics classes. They were little white bread rolls shaped into small bundles of deliciousness. Since then I have experimented with many different breads, some of which can be found in this chapter – such as old-fashioned English muffins, best served hot with loads of butter, the stunning pain d'epi, which often gets oooos and ahhs when brought to the table, and the divine ham, cheese and chive bread, which is ready from start to finish in under an hour.

'Enthusiasm is the yeast that raises the dough.'

Paul J. Meyer

Sea salt & olive oil pain d'epi

The way of shaping this loaf transforms an ordinary baguette into quite a stunner. Place the loaf at the centre of the table so everyone can break off a big hunk. Although there is olive oil in the recipe, I like to serve a little extra oil with a drizzle of balsamic, but it goes really well with butter too. As with most bread, this is best served warm.

Makes 1 loaf *(V)*

275g strong white flour, plus extra for dusting and sprinkling

1 scant tsp sea salt, plus extra for the top

2 tsp fast-action dried yeast

150–185ml warm water

1 tbsp extra-virgin olive oil

Put the flour, 1 teaspoon of salt and the yeast in a large bowl. Add enough of the water to make a lovely soft dough and then the olive oil and mix with a wooden spoon until the mixture begins to come together a little. Put the spoon down and get your hands in, and squidge it together to form a ball. Knead the dough for 10 minutes if doing by hand, or for 5 minutes if using a machine.

Dust a large baking tray with flour, form the dough into a tight ball so that the top is really nice and taut, then roll it into a long and thin baguette shape (thinner than usual, as it will expand while it rises). Cover the tray with oiled clingfilm so it is airtight but not too taut, giving the dough room to expand. Leave it in a warm place for about 1 hour, or until doubled in size. I usually leave mine on a chair near the oven.

Preheat the oven to 200°C (400°F), Gas Mark 6. Once the bread has almost doubled in size, remove the clingfilm and sprinkle over some flour. Put the bread with the shortest edge facing you (or lengthways) and, starting at the end furthest away from you, hold a pair of scissors so they are parallel to the bread, then tilt them so they are at a 45-degree angle. Make a large cut 10cm away from the top of the dough, almost as if you were going to snip that bit off (but it will be attached still), then take that piece and move it to the left. Make another snip about 10cm down from the bottom of the last one and move that piece to the right. Keep on doing this until you reach the end of the bread.

Sprinkle the top with flour and sea salt. Spray some water into the oven to create a steamy atmosphere. I usually spray 8–10 squirts with a spray gun, then place the dough in the oven. Bake for about 25 minutes, or until the bread is cooked. It should smell cooked, be golden brown and sound hollow when you tap it on the bottom.

Twenty-first century ham, cheese & chive bread

On weekends I love to spend hours in the kitchen preparing fresh breads, hearty meat dishes and lots of puddings. I especially love the taste of freshly baked bread! I find that during the week, however, sometimes there just aren't enough hours in the day for baking, so I dreamed up this very tasty little number, which is made from start to finish in under an hour – the perfect 21st-century bread. Makes 1 loaf

- 425g self-raising flour
- 1 tsp baking powder
- ½ tsp salt
- 150g mature Cheddar cheese, grated, plus an extra 10g grated cheese, for sprinkling
- ½ bunch of fresh chives, finely chopped
- Few twists of black pepper
- 1 tsp paprika (optional)
- 1 tsp mustard powder (optional)
- 6 slices of honey roast ham, ripped up into little bits
- 200–225ml water

Preheat the oven to 200°C (400°F), Gas Mark 6. Put all of the ingredients in a bowl except the water and the 10g of grated cheese and mix together well. Add enough water to make a soft but not sticky dough. I usually add 200ml, stir it briefly and then get my hands in and squidge it together, adding more water if necessary. Remove the dough from the bowl and shape it into a ball, flatten the ball slightly, so it cooks more quickly, then slash the loaf three times vertically with a sharp knife. Sprinkle over the remaining grated cheese.

Spray some water into the oven to create a steamy atmosphere. I usually spray 8–10 squirts with a spray gun, then place the dough on a baking tray and bake for 35–45 minutes, or until the bread is golden brown and smells cooked.

Once cooked, remove from the oven and leave to cool a little bit (although I find this quite hard to do!). I love this bread served with lots of butter and a steaming hot bowl of soup.

Old-fashioned English muffins

These beautiful little specimens are truly hard to beat when it comes to the ultimate comfort food. Makes 8–10 muffins *(V)*

575g strong white bread flour

1 tsp salt

1 x 7g sachet of fast-action dried yeast

2 tbsp soft light brown sugar

150ml warm water

175–225ml milk, at room temperature

Oil, for oiling

Equipment

Round pastry cutter; my cutter measured 8.5cm

Put the flour, salt, yeast and sugar in a bowl, then make a well in the centre and pour in the water and milk. Use a wooden spoon to stir it all together, then put the spoon down and use your hands to bring the mixture together into a ball. Knead for 10 minutes by hand or for 5 minutes if using a food processor fitted with a dough hook.

Once it has been kneaded, place the dough in a bowl, cover with oiled clingfilm and leave in a warm place for 1 hour, or until doubled in size.

Preheat the oven to 200°C (400°F), Gas Mark 6. Once the dough is ready, remove it from the bowl and roll it out into a rough circle, about 1.5–2cm thick. Cut out 8–10 circles with the round pastry cutter. Usually when I do these I have to scrunch the dough up and re-roll it so I get the right amount of circles.

Put a flat baking tray or very large frying pan over a low heat. Once the tray or pan is hot, place a few of the circles on the tray or pan and cook slowly for about 4 minutes on each side. It is possible to cook the muffins completely on the hob, but if they have begun to go too dark and are still looking a bit doughy on the sides they can be finished off in the oven for about 5–8 minutes.

Once they are cooked, remove them from the oven/hob and slice in half. I do like to pop these in the toaster or back on the baking tray, cut side down, to crisp up the inside. Then they can be slathered with hot butter and raspberry jam. Totally delicious!

Hamburger baps

I am all for breads with a crunchy crust and am a great advocate of those, but there is also a certain beauty in a soft doughy roll that squidges when lightly pressed. So I embarked on a journey for a soft(ish) roll and found the best way to get one was to use plain flour. If these are cooked for too long, a firm top will result; but if cooked for just the right amount of time, the top will stay soft and squidgy. These baps are great with the salmon and sweet potato fish cakes on page 99, or even the lamb and mint burgers on page 116. When time permits, I double the ingredients and then pop half the baps into the freezer for another day. Makes 5 baps *(V)*

525g plain flour

2 tsp salt

2 tbsp soft light brown sugar

1 x 7g sachet of fast-action dried yeast

150ml warm milk, plus extra for brushing

125–150ml warm water

Sesame seeds

Put the flour, salt, sugar and yeast in bowl. Make a well in the centre and pour in the milk and enough water to make a soft dough. The softer the dough, the better because it will mean the buns will have a really nice rise. Knead the dough for a good 10 minutes if doing by hand and 5 minutes if using a mixer fitted with a dough attachment. To test when the dough is ready, form the dough into a ball so that it has a nice tight top, then using a floured finger, prod it into the dough – if it springs back all the way, then it is ready. Divide the dough into 5 equal portions. Mine weighed 170g each, but this will depend on how much water you have used. Take one portion and shape it into a ball. I like to pull the sides down of the ball down and under so that the top of the bread becomes tight. This makes the bread look really nice when it is cooked.

Now place a dough ball on a baking tray and squash it down a little to flatten it slightly. Repeat with the rest of the dough, placing the dough balls on the tray fairly spaced apart because they will spread during baking. Once all the dough balls are formed, cover them with oiled clingfilm so that it is loose but airtight. I normally have to use several pieces of clingfilm to cover them sufficiently. Leave to rise in a warm place for about 1 hour, or until the dough balls have almost doubled in size.

▶

Preheat the oven to 200°C (400°F), Gas Mark 6. Once the dough balls have risen, carefully remove the clingfilm and brush all over with the extra milk. Sprinkle the sesame seeds over the top. Spray some water into the oven to create a steamy atmosphere. I usually spray 8–10 squirts with a spray gun, then place the baps into the oven. Bake for about 30–35 minutes, or until the baps are golden brown, firm and sound hollow when they are tapped on the bottom. The cooking time will vary according to how much liquid the baps have in them and how long they have been left to rise for.

Once the hamburger baps are cooked, remove them from the oven and leave to cool. These baps are great for burgers, or they can be transformed into iced buns by topping them with icing sugar mixed with a little water.

Puffed-up pitta bread

I LOVE making these! They are so much fun, easy and a real showstopper. These pitta breads have become an absolute firm favourite in my house – wonderful served with curries, dips or soup. Makes 8 pitta breads *(V)*

- 100g wholemeal flour
- 270g plain flour
- 1 tsp salt
- 1 x 7g sachet of fast-action dried yeast
- 1 squidge of honey
- 200–250ml water
- Oil, for oiling

Put all the ingredients into a bowl except the water and oil and stir for a second to combine. Gradually add the water, mixing with a spoon as you go, until you have a soft dough. I used 220ml, but this can differ with how much water there is in the atmosphere! Put your hands in and take the ball of dough out and knead it for 10 minutes until it is very smooth. To test if the dough is ready, prod a floured finger into the side; if it springs back, then it is ready. If you are doing this in a machine, knead with a dough hook for 5 minutes. Once the dough is kneaded, cover it with oiled clingfilm and leave until it is almost doubled in size. This will take about 1 hour or so.

After about 45 minutes preheat the oven to 200°C (400°F), Gas Mark 6 and put a flat baking tray into the oven to heat up. Divide the dough into eight pieces and roll each one out to about the thickness of a £1 coin, then form into a flattish circular or oval shape slightly thicker in the middle than around the sides.

Spray some water into the oven to create a steamy atmosphere. I usually spray 8–10 squirts with a spray gun, then remove the hot tray from the oven and put four of the pittas on it. Slide the tray back into the oven and cook for about 10 minutes, or until the pittas are nicely puffed up and firm, usually about 7–9 minutes depending the thickness of the pitta. Once they are cooked, remove them from the oven, transfer to a plate and pop in the other four.

Occasionally there are one or two pitta breads that do not want to play puffball, but they should puff up beautifully.

Mrs Stephenson's dinner party bread rolls

I first made these during my GCSE Home Economics classes at school. Much to the disdain of my highly academic father, I chose Home Economics over History (but he came round to the idea in the end!). While my friends were learning about Henry VIII, I was staring out of the window of the HE block, kneading my dough with a very, very large grin on my face, dizzy with happiness. One of our first assignments was to make shaped bread rolls, glazed old-school style with a heavy eggwash for maximum shine. The daughter of my Home Economics teacher recently got in touch with me, so Mrs Stephenson, thank you, and this one is for you. Makes 12 rolls *(V)*

280g strong white bread flour, plus extra for dusting

1 tsp salt

1½ tsp fast-action dried yeast

1 tsp soft light brown sugar

190ml warm water

1 egg, lightly beaten, for the eggwash

3 tbsp sesame or poppy seeds

Put the flour, salt, yeast and sugar in a bowl. Then make a well in the centre and pour in the water. Use a wooden spoon to stir it all together, and when it starts getting stiff, put the spoon down and use your hands to squidge it together into a ball. The dough should feel soft and not too hard – like Blu-Tack. If the dough is too stiff, pop it back into the bowl, add a couple of tablespoons of water and squidge it together with your hands until it comes together. Knead for 10 minutes if doing by hand and for 5 minutes in a machine. Once the dough is kneaded, I weigh it and then divide the number by 12, so all the rolls are an even size.

Roll each one into a ball and either just leave them in a ball or shape them as in the photo. Space the rolls on a large baking tray and cover with oiled clingfilm so it is airtight but not too taut. You may need to use two trays. Leave the rolls in a warm place for about 1 hour, or until they are almost doubled in size.

Preheat the oven to 200°C (400°F), Gas Mark 6. To test the dough, remove the clingfilm and with a floured finger, prod the side of the dough – the dent should spring back halfway. Brush liberally all over with the eggwash and sprinkle with the sesame or poppy seeds.

Spray some water into the oven to create a steamy atmosphere. I usually spray 8–10 squirts with a spray gun, then place the rolls into the oven. Bake for about 15–20 minutes, or until they are golden brown and sound hollow when tapped on the bottom.

Spring onion & red chilli cornbread

When you want some and you want it quick, an American-style cornbread spiced with chilli and onion is perfect. Use lots of salt and black pepper in the mix, as this bread needs a good amount of seasoning. Serves 4–5 *(V)*

Oil, for oiling

220g fine cornmeal or polenta

90g plain flour

1 tsp soft light brown sugar

2 tsp bicarbonate of soda

1 egg

200g natural yoghurt

300ml milk

1 tsp salt

75g tinned drained sweetcorn

30g butter or olive oil

3–4 red chillies, finely chopped

1 bunch of spring onions, trimmed and finely sliced

Salt and freshly ground black pepper

Equipment

Medium ovenproof frying pan, a large brownie tin or a 20cm springform tin

Preheat the oven to 220°C (225°F), Gas Mark 7 and oil the pan or tin. If using the springform tin, line the bottom with baking parchment.

Mix all the ingredients together in a large bowl (the mix will look very sloppy and not that appealing, but I promise it will come good), then place the mixture into the pan or tin. Bake in the oven for about 30 minutes, or until the bread looks cooked and is no longer wet.

Once cooked, remove the bread from the oven, leave to cool, then cut into chunks and eat with a hearty soup.

Really quick 'Danish pastries'

When I am thinking of ideas for recipe testing, I lock myself in the kitchen with the television on and a huge pile of ingredients and just experiment. About 1 o'clock one Sunday morning, I was standing in the kitchen and staring at a block of puff pastry that had to be used up. I rifled through the cupboards and fridge and found a small tin of apricots and a little tub of ready-made custard. Within a very short space of time, I had conjured up these 'Danish pastries' – a more than acceptable alternative to the 'proper' ones and with the added satisfaction that they are so quick to make.

Makes 12 small pastries *(V)*

1 x 375g packet of puff pastry

Plain flour, for dusting

1 x 220g tin of apricot halves

300g thick custard (for these I use shop-bought)

1 egg, lightly beaten, for the eggwash

Sugar, for sprinkling

Preheat the oven to 220°C (425°F), Gas Mark 7. Roll out the pastry on a lightly floured work surface to a square 30cm by 30cm. To make the windmill, or what are sometimes called Imperial stars, cut the pastry into 7.5cm squares and make diagonal cuts from each corner to within 1cm of the centre. Put one or two apricot halves in the centre of the square and spoon over a little ready-made thick vanilla custard, then fold alternate corners of each cut section down to the centre, brushing the tips with beaten egg.

Place them into the fridge for 15 minutes or so until they are firm. Remove them from the fridge, brush them with eggwash and sprinkle with sugar, then place the pastries into the oven. Bake for about 20–25 minutes, or until they are firm, risen and golden brown.

Remove them from the oven and leave to cool.

Mains

There is always a question in my mind at the beginning of every day – and that is, what shall I serve for dinner? At the weekends, this also becomes, what shall I serve for lunch? Most days I get in the kitchen and whip up something for the family, but I will wholeheartedly put my hands in the air and say that some days I pop out to the local supermarket and buy something out of a packet to prick with a fork and bung in the oven. So, I wanted to come up with a chapter full of recipes to cook for a main meal, such as super-fast pan-fried lemon sole, to the slightly less quick but very much worth the wait slow-roast pork shoulder with crispy crackling and the very frequently made (in my house) not-so-Cornish pasties. However much time you have, and no matter what the occasion, there is much to choose from here, whether you're planning a family meal or a smart dinner to impress.

'An empty belly is the best cook.'

Estonian proverb

Decadent rosemary & Worcestershire sauce shepherd's pie

This pie is an old-school classic with a hint of something extra. Serves 4–6

- Oil, for cooking
- 2 medium red onions, peeled and chopped
- 3–4 tbsp balsamic vinegar
- 2 carrots, peeled and cut into small cubes
- 1 stick of celery, trimmed and chopped (optional)
- 2 sprigs of fresh rosemary, finely chopped
- 700–750g lamb mince
- 2 large squidges of tomato purée
- 3–4 tbsp Worcestershire sauce
- 200ml Madeira or a good red wine or lamb or beef stock
- Salt and freshly ground black pepper
- 1 bay leaf

Heat some oil in a large pan, add the onions and cook for a few minutes until they are soft. Add the balsamic vinegar, turn up the heat and cook until all the vinegar has evaporated – this adds a little extra flavour. Add the carrots, celery, if using, and rosemary, then stir it all together and cook for a couple of minutes. Add the lamb mince, break it up with a wooden spoon and cook it until the meat has turned from pink to brown.

Preheat the oven to 180°C (350°F), Gas Mark 4. Add the tomato purée, Worcestershire sauce, wine or stock, salt and pepper and the bay leaf and simmer for 30 minutes.

Meanwhile, for the mashed potato, put a large pan of salted water on to boil. Cover with the lid so it comes to the boil faster. Once it is boiling, add the potatoes and cook for 10–20 minutes, or until they are nice and tender and a knife can glide through them easily.

Drain the potatoes, then return them to the pan. Using a potato masher or mouli, mash the potatoes until smooth, then add the cream, butter, salt, pepper and nutmeg, if using, and mix well together. If the mashed potatoes have gone cold, then return the pan to the hob and heat over a medium heat. Make a well in the centre of the potatoes, drop in the butter and wait until it melts, then remove the pan from the heat and add the rest of the ingredients, mixing well. Taste, adjust the seasoning, add more butter if needed, then set aside.

▶

Decadent rosemary & Worcestershire sauce shepherd's pie (continued)

Mashed potato

1kg mashing potatoes, peeled and cut into large chunks

70ml single cream

75g butter

Freshly grated nutmeg (optional)

Grated cheese and breadcrumbs, for sprinkling (optional)

Equipment

Medium casserole dish

Piping bag fitted with a star nozzle

Tip the meat mixture into the casserole dish. If you find that there is too much liquid at this stage, use a slotted spoon to transfer the meat to the casserole dish. This lovely leftover gravy can be used to pour over the shepherd's pie once it is cooked.

Dollop the mash on top and fork it through to make a pattern. I like to allow the mash to cool a bit, then put it into the piping bag fitted with a star nozzle and pipe the mash on top. Cook the shepherd's pie in the oven for 20–30 minutes. While not strictly authentic, a large handful each of grated cheese and breadcrumbs sprinkled over the top prior to baking is a delicious optional extra.

Serve with a crispy and crunchy green salad.

Lemon, tarragon & garlic quick roast chicken with oven-baked potato slices

This is the best way to cook a chicken when time is not on your side, because the chicken is cooked flat it needs less cooking time, so the bird stays beautifully moist.
Serves 4

5 medium potatoes
1 bulb of garlic, unpeeled
Oil, for drizzling and rubbing
Salt and freshly ground black pepper
About 1.5kg chicken (preferably free range)
2 pinches of mustard powder
1 lemon, finely sliced
¼ bunch of fresh tarragon leaves
1 glass of Marsala or wine
1 tbsp plain flour
1 mugful of chicken stock
Caster sugar (optional)

Preheat the oven to 220°C (425°F), Gas Mark 7. Arrange the potatoes in a single layer (as much as is possible) in a large baking tray. Bash a garlic clove and add it to the potatoes, then drizzle with a little oil, season with salt and pepper and bake in the oven for 45 minutes.

Turn the chicken breast-side down and, using a good pair of scissors, cut along the side of the backbone (not right on it) from one end to the other so that the bird opens up flat. Now turn the chicken breast side up, place your hand on the breastbone and push down firmly until there is a small crack – this will help the bird to lie down nice and flat – and then place it in a roasting tin.

Rub the chicken with some oil and sprinkle over the mustard powder. Scatter the lemon slices over the chicken and sprinkle over the remaining garlic cloves. Sprinkle half of the tarragon over and season well with salt and pepper. Roast in the oven for about 45–50 minutes, or until the chicken is completely cooked (the cooking time will depend on the size and temperature of the bird when it was put in the oven). To test that the chicken is cooked, insert a sharp knife into the thickest part of the leg, then press the knife down a little; if the juices run clear and are no longer bloody, the chicken is cooked.

▶

Lemon, tarragon & garlic quick roast chicken with oven-baked potato slices (continued)

Five minutes before the chicken is ready, pop a plate in the oven. This can be used to put the chicken on when it is left to rest. Remove the cooked chicken from the oven along with the warmed plate, then remove the chicken and lemon slices from the roasting tin, discarding the lemon slices. Place the chicken on the plate and cover with foil to keep warm. If the potatoes are cooked, remove them from the oven.

Tip off all but 1 tablespoon of the roasting juices from the tin, add the wine and place the tin on the hob over a high heat, scraping off any bits of chicken left at the bottom of the pan. Bring the juices to the boil and boil until reduced by half. Add the flour slowly, stirring all the time, then add the stock together with the rest of the tarragon leaves. Boil for a few minutes until the sauce thickens, then remove the pan from the heat. Taste and check that it is just the way you like it, adding salt, pepper, or even a pinch of sugar to get it just right.

I usually serve the chicken by cutting it up into portions with scissors, as it is much easier than using a knife when it is split open. Place some potatoes on the serving plate with a chicken portion on top and finished off with some sauce.

Cracked black pepper pasta

Undeniably it is faster to buy shop-bought pasta than make your own, but there is something very rewarding about seeing these white strands of pasta speckled with black hanging all round the kitchen! Serves 4–5 *(V)*

400g '00' flour, plus extra for dusting

4 eggs

1 tbsp olive oil, plus extra for drizzling

1–2 tbsp cracked black pepper

Few fresh basil leaves, for sprinkling

Equipment

Coat hangers

Pasta machine (optional)

Get a couple of coat hangers ready, which have been cleaned and wiped. Hang them on the cupboard handles, ready to hang the pasta on.

Put all the ingredients into a food processor and blitz until they resemble breadcrumbs, then tip the mixture onto the work surface and knead it lightly for a few minutes to form a ball of dough. The dough should be quite stiff and smooth. Wrap the dough in clingfilm and leave to rest at room temperature for 30 minutes.

If making the pasta by machine, take about a quarter of the pasta and squish the pasta as flat as you can with your hands, then feed it through the widest possible setting on the pasta machine. Fold it into a rectangle shape and feed it through again. Lower the width setting one notch and feed it through again, then lower it another notch and feed it through again. After you have fed it through on the initial setting, there is no need to keep folding it; just keep feeding it through, making the setting narrower each time. If the pasta rips while using the pasta machine, don't worry, just fold it back into a rectangle and feed it through the widest setting again. A rip may mean that there is an obstruction in the pasta machine between the rollers. If that is the case, just open the machine to the widest setting and let whatever was stuck in there fall out. If the pasta sticks to the machine, just flour the machine a little to help ease the pasta through.

▶

Cracked black pepper pasta
(continued)

When you have fed the pasta through on the narrowest setting, sprinkle the top with a little flour and fold it in half, short end to short end, then again, and again and again until you have a smaller rectangle. With the folded edge facing you, cut vertical strips about 1–2cm wide along the width of the pasta, then carefully take one strip, unfold it completely and hang it on the coat hanger. Repeat with the rest of the pasta, using a quarter piece of the dough each time.

If making the pasta by hand, dust the work surface very lightly with flour. Take a quarter of the dough and put it on the work surface. Squish the dough into a flattish rectangle shape and roll it out until it is a very long and thin rectangle. My rectangle was 12–15cm wide and very, very long. The pasta is ready when it is so thin that if you lift it up and put your hand behind it, you can see your hand through it. Sprinkle the top with a little flour and fold it in half, short end to short end, then again, and again and again until you have a smaller rectangle. With the folded edge facing you, cut vertical strips about 1–2cm wide along the width of the pasta. Carefully take one strip and unfold it and hang it on the coat hanger. Repeat with the rest of the pasta, using a quarter piece at a time.

Once all of the pasta is hung, bring a large pan of salted water to the boil. As soon as the water is boiling, add the pasta in one or two batches, depending on how big your pan is, and cook for about 4–5 minutes. Using a pair of tongs, remove the pasta from the pan and, drain in a colander. If cooking the pasta in batches keep the first batch warm while cooking the rest.

Once all the pasta is cooked and drained, drizzle with some olive oil and sprinkle a few basil leaves over the top, then serve immediately. This is delicious served with creamy pancetta sauce (see page 88) or lemony basil and mascarpone sauce (see page 162).

Really slow-roast pork shoulder with crispy, crispy crackling & garlic roast vegetables

Really, easy peasy pork; this isn't the fastest dish in the world, but it is super simple and the crackling is definitely worth the wait. Serves 4–6

2 tsp fennel seeds

Few black peppercorns

1 x 2kg boneless pork shoulder joint with rind slashed

4–5 large potatoes, peeled and cut into plum-size pieces

5 cloves of garlic, unpeeled

6–8 shallots, peeled and left whole or 1 large onion, peeled and cut into 6 chunks

3 carrots, peeled and cut into large pieces

2 large pears, cut into quarters

Preheat the oven to 160°C (315°F), Gas Mark 2–3. Grind the fennel seeds with the peppercorns and some salt.

Place the pork shoulder joint in a roasting tin, rub the rind with the ground fennel seed mixture and cook in the oven for 6 hours. After 4 hours, remove the pork from the oven and arrange the potatoes around and underneath the meat, then put it back in the oven.

After 5 hours, put the rest of the vegetables around the pork and return to the oven. If your roasting tin is not large enough to accommodate the vegetables and the pork together, just place them in a separate roasting tin. Thirty minutes before the pork is ready, throw in the pears, as they don't need much cooking time and will just disintegrate if cooked for too long.

Once the meat is cooked and flakes away with a fork, remove it and the vegetables from the pan and keep warm. This will give the pork time to rest and become more tender. If the pork does not have crispy crackling, put it under the grill for a moment or two until really crunchy and crispy.

Really slow-roast pork shoulder with crispy, crispy crackling & garlic roast vegetables (continued)

Gravy

1 heaped tbsp flour

1 glass of white wine (optional)

275–300ml good-quality chicken stock

Salt and freshly ground black pepper

For the gravy, pour off all but about 1 tablespoon of the fat from the roasting tin. Add the flour and stir in. Place the roasting tin on the hob, add the wine, if using, and boil until the wine is reduced by over a half. Add the stock and put it over a high heat and boil it like mad until it starts to thicken, scraping off any bits of meat or vegetables on the bottom of the tin. Taste and add any seasoning if you think it needs it. If your gravy is too thin, make a paste with a blob of butter and a tablespoon of flour in a mug, then add 2 tablespoons of the hot gravy mix and stir into a paste. Add the paste to the hot stock, stirring constantly, then bring to the boil – the gravy will thicken slightly. If your gravy is too thick, just add a touch more stock.

Serve the meat and vegetables with the gravy.

This dish struggles to make it to the table, as the family descend upon it while I am trying to finish off the gravy! Use any leftovers for pork sandwiches, served with some crunchy brown pickle.

Five-spice baked ribs

So, very very tasty and super easy, this is messy, sticky finger food. For me, they are exquisite! Serves 3–4

About 800g–1kg pork spare ribs

½ bunch of spring onions, trimmed and chopped

Salt and freshly ground black pepper

Rub

1 star anise

1 tsp fennel seeds

Few whole Szechuan pepper

1 tbsp five-spice powder

Salt

Sticky honey glaze

2 tbsp olive oil

Few squidges of honey

1–2 cloves of garlic, peeled and finely chopped

150ml soy sauce

Grated zest of 1 lime

3 tbsp sesame seeds (optional)

1–2 red chillies, deseeded and finely sliced

Preheat the oven to 200°C (400°F), Gas Mark 6. Place some foil on the base of a large baking tray or roasting tin (this dish gets quite messy!).

Crush the star anise, fennel seeds and Szechuan pepper in a pestle and mortar, then put in a small bowl, add the five-spice powder and some salt and mix together to combine.

Put the ribs in a bowl and sprinkle over the rub mix. I like to get my hands in and rub everything in, then tip the ribs onto the baking tray and spread them out in a single layer. Cook in the oven for 45 minutes.

Meanwhile, mix all the ingredients for the honey glaze in a small pan. After 45 minutes, take the ribs from the oven and brush with the honey glaze generously, then sprinkle with the spring onions and season well with salt and pepper. Set the rest of the honey glaze aside for later.

Return the ribs to the oven and cook for a further 15 minutes.

Once the ribs are cooked, remove them from the oven and tip them onto a large plate. Reheat the remaining sticky glaze and serve as a dipping sauce with the ribs and a large green salad. I like to serve everything in the middle of the table so everyone can help themselves.

Beer-battered fish & baked chunky chips

I wanted to develop the perfect batter for this dish. I ended up covered in flour with bowls of mixture everywhere at 2am one morning until I found that eureka moment – the perfect batter! This batter is crisp and very tasty. Seeing as it needs to rest for an hour, there is plenty of time to make some delicious homemade chips. Serves 4

- 260g self-raising flour
- 4 tbsp cornflour
- ¼ tsp fast-action dried yeast
- Salt and freshly ground black pepper
- 350ml good lager
- 1kg potatoes, peeled
- About 800ml vegetable oil, plus extra for drizzling
- Plain flour, for dusting
- 4 chunky fish fillets, such as haddock, cod or pollack (preferably sustainably caught)
- 1 lemon or lime, cut into quarters

Put the flour, cornflour, yeast and a large pinch of salt in a bowl. Make a well in the centre of the mixture and gradually add the lager, stirring all the time to make sure there are no lumps. Cover and leave the batter for 1 hour to allow the starch to swell to give a lighter batter.

Preheat the oven to 220°C (425°F), Gas Mark 7. Bring a pan of salted water to the boil. Slice the potatoes into 1cm pieces and then cut each slice into 1–2cm strips. Place the potatoes into the boiling water and boil for 2–3 minutes. Drain the potatoes and pat them dry. Arrange them in a single layer on a large baking tray and drizzle with a little oil. Season well with salt and pepper and cook in the oven for 15 minutes. Take them out of the oven, give them a good shake to move them about and return them to the oven for a further 15 minutes, or until the chips are nice and crisp.

About 15 minutes or so before the chips are ready, heat the oil for deep-frying in a deep pan over a medium heat until a small piece of bread carefully dropped into the oil browns in about 50–55 seconds. Once it is almost at this stage, season the plain flour with salt and pepper, then dip the fish in the seasoned flour and then into the batter. Shake off a little of the excess, carefully lower it into the hot oil and deep-fry for about 5–6 minutes (depending on the thickness of your fish). Remove and leave to drain on a wire rack with a piece of kitchen paper underneath. Repeat with the rest of the fish.

Serve the fish with the hot chips and lemon quarters. Fish and chips to me are not fish and chips without loads of malt vinegar and a good squeeze of ketchup.

Pad Thai

Several years ago I embarked on a six-week culinary tour of Southeast Asia, starting in Northern Thailand with my daughter. We then travelled to Laos down the Mekong to Luang Prabang and then flew to Vietnam and made our way south from Hanoi to Ho Chi Minh City, into Cambodia and finishing off back in Thailand. We cooked frequently in each country, taking classes in grand colonial hotels and humble homestays, learning about the different flavours and specialities of each country and indeed each region. We ate deep-fried insects and learnt to eat chillies hot enough to make you cry.

I recently visited Thailand again and as soon as I had touched down I was straight out on the streets scouring for a quaint eatery in which to eat my all-time favourite Thai dish – pad Thai. This noodle dish is pure class – you can use chicken, beef or vegetables. If you are using meat, cook it for a wee bit longer than the prawns. Serves 2–3

- 2 tbsp oil
- 2 eggs, lightly beaten
- ½ bunch of spring onions, trimmed and finely sliced
- 220g raw tiger prawns, peeled with tails intact
- 100ml water
- 400g straight-to-wok egg noodles
- 3 tbsp caster sugar
- A pinch of salt
- 1 tbsp soy sauce
- 1 tbsp oyster sauce
- 100g beansprouts
- 1 large handful of peanuts, toasted for a few minutes in a pan, then crushed (not the dry-roasted kind)
- 3–4 small red and green chillies, finely chopped
- 3 tbsp tamarind paste
- Squeeze of lime, or to taste

Heat a little oil in a frying pan or wok over a medium heat. Crack in the eggs, breaking up the yolks and whites, then quickly swirl around the pan and cook a thin omelette. Remove from the pan or wok by flipping onto a plate or board and slice into thin shreds, then set aside. Add a little more oil to the pan, add the spring onions and cook for 2 minutes. Add a tiny splash more oil, then add the prawns and cook for 2–3 minutes, or until they begin to turn pink.

Add the water and noodles (you may need to add a little more water depending on the noodles you are using) and cook until the noodles are soft.

Add the sugar, salt, soy sauce, oyster sauce, beansprouts, a large handful of roasted peanuts, chillies and tamarind paste. Cook for a further 3 minutes. Add the shredded omelette and mix gently to heat through. Taste the mixture, add a squeeze of lime and see if you need to add anything else, then serve.

Thai green chicken curry

My second-favourite Thai dish and fast becoming the curry of choice in the UK is green chicken curry. It is so very easy to make, and once you have mastered the simple art of a Thai green chicken curry you will always want to make your own. The beauty lies in being able to add just the right amount of curry paste and fish sauce and the perfect amount of chilli. Serves 4 small portions

Drizzle of vegetable oil

3 tbsp green curry paste

4 skinless, boneless chicken breasts or 6 skinless, boneless chicken thighs, cut into bite-sized chunks

1 x 400ml tin of coconut milk

100ml water

½ small aubergine, cut into bite-sized chunks or 2 handfuls of frozen peas

2 tsp sugar

Pinch of salt

1 tbsp fish sauce

2 kaffir lime leaves

Small handful of fresh basil leaves

1 medium red chilli, deseeded and finely chopped, to garnish

Heat the oil in a large frying pan over a medium–high heat, add the green curry paste and cook until you can begin to smell all those spicy flavours, about 2 minutes. Add the chicken and cook for 5 minutes or so until the chicken pieces are almost cooked through, then pour in the coconut milk and water.

Turn up the heat and let the mixture bubble away for 3–4 minutes. Add the aubergine or peas, reduce the heat and leave to simmer for a further 5 minutes.

Now add the sugar, salt and fish sauce, stir it all together and taste to see if the flavours are just right for you. Add the kaffir lime leaves and basil, then take the pan off the heat. Sprinkle over the chopped chilli to garnish and serve with a steaming pile of fluffy white rice.

Oven-roast salmon with a mustard & parsley crust

I have made this dish for myself when eating alone in the evening and also when friends come round for dinner. It is super fast and really easy to do, and the combination of flavours is very tasty. Serves 4

100g dried breadcrumbs

1½ tbsp soft light brown sugar

2 tbsp Dijon mustard

Knob of butter

Grated zest of 2–3 limes (use the limes to squeeze over the baked fish)

1 bunch of fresh parsley, finely chopped

Salt and freshly ground black pepper

4 skinless salmon or trout fillets (preferably sustainably caught)

Preheat the oven to 200°C (400°F), Gas Mark 6. Mix the breadcrumbs, sugar, mustard, butter, lime zest, parsley and seasoning together in a small bowl. Divide the mixture among the 4 fish fillets and pat the mixture on top of each one. You will need to squish it down so it sticks. Don't worry if some of the mixture falls off the side.

Put the fish in an ovenproof dish, then place it in the oven and bake for 10–15 minutes (depending on how you like your fish cooked). Once cooked, take out of the oven, transfer to warmed serving plates and serve with steaming hot boiled potatoes and broccoli, both tossed in a little butter.

I love to eat this with good Swiss chard, too.

Rosemary & sage pork chops with caramelised shallots & cider

A quick supper dish that I make over and over again. Serves 4

Mashed potato

4 large potatoes, peeled and cut into large chunks

75ml double cream (or milk works too)

2 tbsp grainy mustard

Large knob of butter

Chops

Large knob of butter

2 tbsp caster sugar

2 apples, peeled, cored and cut into small cubes

Oil, for cooking

6 shallots, peeled and finely diced

2 sprigs of fresh rosemary, finely chopped

4 pork chops

1 clove of garlic, peeled and finely chopped

1 glass of dry cider

A few fresh sage leaves, finely chopped (optional)

150ml double cream

Salt and freshly ground black pepper

Put the potatoes into a large pan, pop them on to boil and leave them to cook while you get on with the chops.

Now put the butter and sugar in a pan over a medium heat and stir until the butter has melted and the sugar has dissolved. Throw in the apples, then turn up the heat to high and cook for about 5 minutes, stirring from time to time.

Tip the apples into a bowl, allow the pan to cool a little, then rinse and dry the pan. Put the pan back on the heat with some oil, add the shallots and fry for about 5 minutes, or until the shallots have softened. Tip them into the bowl with the apples.

Spread out half of the chopped rosemary on a chopping board and season well with salt and pepper. Place the chops on top and press down well so that the herbs and seasoning stick to the chops. Season the top of the meat with salt and pepper and sprinkle the rest of the rosemary over the top, pressing it down so the flavour gets into the meat.

Put some oil in the frying pan or sauté pan and heat until hot. When the oil is sizzling, place the chops in the pan and cook for 5–7 minutes, or until they have a good golden brown colour on one side. Now flip the chops over and cook for a further 5–7 minutes on the other side.

While the chops are cooking, drain the potatoes and place them back in the pan. Use a potato masher or mouli to mash the potatoes, then stir in the cream or milk, lots of salt and pepper and the mustard. Pop a lid on the mash to keep warm. Once the pork chops are cooked (they should be piping hot in the middle), transfer them to a plate, cover with foil and keep warm.

▶

Pour off any excess fat from the pan, then add the garlic and cook for about 30 seconds. Add the cider and turn up the heat. If there are any crunchy bits of meat left on the bottom of the pan, use a wooden spoon to scrape these off. Boil the cider until it is reduced by half, then add the sage, if using, and the cream and boil a little so that the sauce begins to thicken. Throw the apples and onions into the pan and cook for 1 minute to reheat. Take the pan off the heat and allow the sauce to cool for a moment, then check the seasoning.

I put a huge dollop of the steaming mustard mash down first, then a pork chop on top with a good drizzling of the sauce to finish.

Quick brown sugar & spring onion chicken teriyaki

Personally I find the flavour of thighs and legs much more appealing than chicken breasts, but every time I try to make a dish at home with them, someone is not happy and the chicken breast reigns supreme again! It is, however, a really nice quick and simple dish which is great served with some perfectly cooked white rice. Serves 4

50g soft light brown sugar

80ml mirin

65g soy sauce

Oil, for pan-frying

3–4 skinless chicken breasts, cut into bite-size chunks or 6–8 boneless chicken thighs

Salt and freshly ground black pepper

1x 2cm piece of fresh ginger, peeled and grated

1 garlic clove, peeled and finely chopped

1 small bunch of spring onions, trimmed and finely sliced on the diagonal

Handful of sesame seeds, toasted (fry in a dry frying pan for 2–3 minutes until golden brown; keep a good eye on them because they burn easily)

Make sure you have everything ready so it can all be thrown into the pan as needed. Put the sugar, mirin and soy sauce in one bowl. Put some oil in a frying pan over a medium heat. Season the chicken really well with some salt and pepper and once the oil is hot enough, add the chicken to the pan and fry for 2 minutes. Add the ginger and garlic and cook for a further minute.

Tip in the sugar, mirin and soy sauce mixture and simmer for 3–5 minutes to thicken slightly (the sauce will still be quite thin), then add the spring onions and cook for 2 minutes. Take the pan off the heat, throw in the toasted sesame seeds and serve immediately with some quick-cook rice and a crispy green salad.

Stove-top haddock with fennel seeds & basil

While wandering around the aisles of my local supermarket perusing the shelves, I came across tinned cherry tomatoes – I am now totally hooked. They are a little bit sweeter than our large plum tomato friends, and a complete joy to use. This super-fast dish is great for a family supper. I am a fennel fan, but do leave the fennel out if you are not keen. Serves 4

- Oil, for cooking
- 1 large red onion, peeled and finely chopped
- 2 cloves of garlic, peeled and chopped
- 2 x 400g tins of cherry tomatoes
- 1 tbsp caster sugar
- Salt and freshly ground black pepper
- 1 bay leaf
- 1 tsp fennel seeds
- 4 haddock fillets, about 500g in total (preferably sustainably caught), skin removed
- Handful of fresh basil leaves

Put some oil in a sauté pan over a low heat, add the onion and cook for 5–7 minutes, or until the onion is nice and soft with no crunch. Add the garlic and cook for another minute. Pour in the cherry tomatoes, sugar, salt and pepper, bay leaf and fennel seeds and cook for a further 2 minutes. Add the haddock fillets, spooning the mixture all over them, then cover with a lid and cook for about 8 minutes, or until the haddock is piping hot in the centre.

Take the pan off the heat, leave to cool a little before tasting and adjust the seasoning if you think it needs it. Rip up the basil leaves and add to the fish, stir lightly and serve.

I like to serve this with some fluffy white rice.

Creamy pancetta pasta with mushrooms & Parmesan

This dish is a perfect quick-fix solution for a weekday dinner and is one of the easiest pasta sauce recipes I know. Serve with the homemade cracked black pepper pasta on page 64, or for an even quicker option, use shop-bought. Serves 4

400g papardelle or 1 x recipe homemade pasta

100–200g cubed pancetta

175g chestnut mushrooms, wiped and finely sliced

225ml double cream

75g grated Parmesan cheese

Freshly ground black pepper

Cook the pasta according to the manufacturer's instructions or the recipe on page 64 if using homemade.

Meanwhile, put the pancetta in a medium pan over a medium to high heat. When it starts to go brown, add the mushrooms and cook for about 2–3 minutes, then add the double cream. Once the cream is hot, add the Parmesan and stir together well.

Once the pasta is ready, drain and then return it to the pan. Add the creamy mixture and stir through well. Season with some pepper (I find it does not usually need salt because of the salty Parmesan and pancetta). Serve piping hot with a rocket salad.

ROYAL VICTORIA YACHT CLUB

Simple pan-fried lemon sole with parsley & browned butter

I have to say, this is one of my all-time favourite fish dishes. It is ready in seconds and the flavour is totally out of this world. I was not the most confident person with fish, and this particular fish is delicate and not easy to get right. Once I realised lemon sole needs just a momentary quick flash in the pan, however, my confidence grew and grew. Now I cook this fish at least once a week, almost every week of the year. Serves 4

4 good-sized sole fillets (preferably sustainably caught)

Salt and freshly ground black pepper

80–90g butter

1 plateful of plain flour

Handful of fresh parsley, finely chopped

Juice of 1 lemon

If you would like to skin the fish, put the fillet skin side down on a plate with the thinnest end pointing towards you. I put a little salt on the very end, as this makes it easier to grip. Using a sharp knife, preferably with a thin flexible blade, make a slit at the thin end at a 45-degree angle so that the knife is between the skin and the flesh. Now keeping the knife at a slight angle, use a gentle sawing motion to move the knife away from you towards the thicker end of the fillet until the skin is removed.

Preheat the oven to 110°C (225°F), Gas Mark ¼ and place 4 plates inside to heat. Put a large frying pan over a medium heat and add a quarter of the butter. While the butter is melting, season the plate of flour with salt and pepper, then dip the sole fillets into the seasoned flour. Pat the flour all over it so the fish is well covered and shake off the excess.

Once the butter is sizzling and piping hot, place two fillets in the pan and fry for 30 seconds on each side. Take the pan off the heat and take the plates out the oven. Put the cooked fish on the plates and cover loosely with foil to keep warm. Now repeat with the other fillets.

Carefully wipe out the pan with some kitchen paper and put the empty frying pan back on the heat. Add the rest of the butter and cook for a minute or so until it has gone a medium golden brown colour. Add the parsley and cook for 2 seconds, then divide the butter among the plates. Squeeze over a generous amount of lemon juice and serve.

I like to serve this dish with boiled crushed new potatoes mixed with a dollop of crème fraîche, a squeeze of lime juice, salt and pepper, a sprinkling of fresh herbs and a crisp green salad.

Warm & cosy coq au vin

This chicken stew is like a great big hug on those days when you really need it.

Serves 4

- 15g dried porcini mushrooms
- Oil, for cooking
- Plain flour, for dusting
- Salt and freshly ground black pepper
- 8 chicken pieces, thighs and legs are best
- 140g pancetta pieces
- 8–10 small shallots
- Few sprigs of fresh thyme
- Few sprigs of fresh rosemary, woody stem removed and leaves finely chopped
- 1 bay leaf
- I clove of garlic, squashed
- 150g chestnut mushrooms, wiped and finely sliced
- 2 tbsp flour
- 550ml good red wine
- 400ml chicken stock
- 1 carrot, peeled and chopped into sticks
- 1 handful of fresh parsley, roughly chopped

Soak the dried porcini mushrooms in a bowl of hot water for 20 minutes. Drain, saving the soaking liquid for later, just in case it's needed, and roughly chop the mushrooms, then set aside.

Heat some oil in a sauté pan or frying pan until it is nice and hot. Meanwhile, season the flour well with salt and pepper. Toss the chicken pieces in the seasoned flour and put half of them in the pan, if the pan is big enough, and brown all over. Once the chicken pieces are nicely browned, transfer them to a plate and repeat with the rest of the chicken, then set them aside.

Put the pancetta pieces in the pan and fry until they are beginning to crisp, then tip them onto the plate with the chicken. Add the shallots and fry for a minute or so, then add the thyme, rosemary, bay leaf, garlic and mushrooms and cook until the mushrooms begin to soften, adding more oil if needed. Add the flour and stir to mix everything together. Continue to stir, then gradually add the wine together with the stock. Once all the liquid has been added, return all the chicken pieces and pancetta to the pan along with the reserved porcini mushrooms and cook for 20–25 minutes (40 if they are large pieces), or until the juices of the chicken run clear when a skewer is inserted into the thickest part of the meat, and the meat is cooked. Ten minutes before the chicken is ready, add the carrots.

If the stew is too runny, put a sieve over a bowl, tip the chicken into it, and put the bowl with the liquid in back over the heat (and a plate under the chicken to catch the juices!). Boil like mad to reduce. If there is not enough sauce, add a bit of the reserved porcini soaking liquid and/or some stock and heat through. Serve sprinkled with chopped parsley.

Pot-roast beef with port & juniper berries

Pot-roast beef is a simple alternative to a traditional roast beef lunch, especially served with Yorkshire puddings. Traditional pot roasting is done without any liquid and the joint is roasted in a pot with a tight-fitting lid on a bed of vegetables, but I have broken with tradition and added port for good measure. The supermarkets sell brisket, topside or top rump (but this is better for just plain roasting) and silverside. I have found the best joints for this are brisket or silverside. Juniper berries are found in most supermarkets in the dried herbs and spices section. Serves 4

Oil, for cooking

About 1.3kg brisket or silverside

Salt and freshly ground black pepper

2 large carrots, peeled and cut into large chunks

2 red onions, peeled and cut into large chunks

1–2 tbsp plain flour

450ml port or 450ml good liquid beef stock

1 bay leaf

2 juniper berries

Handful of black peppercorns

1 tsp tomato purée

1 tbsp brown sugar

Equipment

Large casserole dish, preferably with a tight-fitting lid

Preheat the oven to 150°C (300°F), Gas Mark 5. Put some oil in a frying pan over a medium–high heat. Season the meat with lots of salt and pepper, add to the pan and brown well on all sides. Then transfer the meat to a plate. Put the carrots and the onions in the pan, adding a little more oil if necessary, and cook until browned. Add a bit of flour, stir and put them with the beef. Tip off any excess oil and allow the pan to cool a little, then wipe out any remaining oil. Pour the port, if using, into the pan and boil like mad over a high heat for 5 minutes, just enough to get rid of the strong alcohol taste, then take off the heat.

Put the vegetables in the base of the casserole dish and place the beef on top. Pour in the port or stock and all the other ingredients. Scrunch up some greaseproof paper or foil, then unscrunch it and lay it on top of the meat so it overlaps the sides a little. Cover with a tight-fitting lid. If you do not have a lid that fits, just put a flat baking tray over the top, then weigh it down with a cake tin filled with baking beans. Cook in the oven for 3 hours.

Once the meat is cooked, remove the casserole dish from the oven, take the beef joint out of the sauce and place it on a plate. Cover with a piece of greaseproof paper and keep warm.

If the juices look too thin, pour them into a frying pan, bring to the boil and boil until they thicken, about 5–10 minutes depending on how thick you would like the sauce. Serve the sauce with the beef and some goose-fat roast potatoes.

Rack of lamb with a rosemary & parsley pesto crust

This rack of lamb is a gorgeous dinner party classic, and is the ultimate dish to prepare if you are in a hurry. Serves 4

Oil, for cooking

3 x 6–7-bone racks of lamb, well-trimmed

Salt and freshly ground black pepper

2 tbsp English mustard

Pesto

2 sprigs of fresh rosemary, leaves only, finely chopped

1 small bunch of fresh parsley

75g grated Parmesan cheese

30ml extra-virgin olive oil

1 small garlic clove

Freshly ground black pepper

Handful of breadcrumbs

Pinch of grated lemon zest

Preheat the oven to 200°C (400°F), Gas Mark 6. Heat the oil in a frying pan. Slash the fat on the lamb racks (if there is any) and season them very well with salt and pepper. Take a couple of the racks and brown them quickly in the pan until they are browned all over. Remove them from the heat and put them on a plate. Repeat with the rest of the racks, only doing a couple at a time so as not to overcrowd the pan. Put the racks into a roasting tin (unless you have an ovenproof frying pan) and cook in the oven for about 10 minutes.

Meanwhile, make the pesto. Place all the ingredients in a blender and blitz together. If you do not have a blender, you can mash all the ingredients together, then tip into a bowl and set aside.

Remove the lamb from the oven and, using a pastry brush, coat with the mustard. Dip the lamb into the pesto mix, pressing the green mixture all over the meat, then return the racks to the oven for a further 5 minutes for rare, 5–10 minutes for medium and 10–15 minutes for well done. Remove from the oven and leave in a warm place for 8–10 minutes to rest before serving.

Sweet potato & salmon fish cakes with chives & lime

I cracked open one of these sweet potatoes recently to be greeted with an exotic-looking orange flesh. Adding sweet potatoes to this recipe really makes the difference, so seek them out where you can. Trout is a lesser-used fish in the UK, but it is a delicious alternative and often somewhat cheaper than salmon. Serves 4

500ml vegetable or fish stock (water with a few peppercorns and bay leaf is also fine)

400g sweet potato, peeled and diced (about 3 smallish ones)

200–250g salmon or trout fillets, skin removed and each one cut in half (sustainably caught)

Large pinch of paprika

Squeeze of lime juice

1 bunch of fresh chives, finely chopped

Salt and freshly ground black pepper

1 egg, lightly beaten

Oil, for shallow-frying or oiling

1 lime, cut into quarters, to garnish (optional)

Coating

1 egg, lightly beaten

100g dried breadcrumbs

These fish cakes can either be shallow-fried in a little oil for 2–3 minutes, or they can be baked for 20–30 minutes. If you are using the oven method, preheat the oven to 180°C (350°F), Gas Mark 4.

Pour the stock into a sauté pan and bring to the boil. Add the sweet potato chunks and fish and cover with a lid. Cook for about 10 minutes (although this may vary according to the thickness of your fish) until the sweet potato and salmon are cooked. You can tell that the fish is cooked because the flesh will be very shiny inside and will be the same colour all the way through. The sweet potato should be nicely cooked through and 'give' easily when a knife is inserted into it. Take the pan off the heat and drain well into a colander set in the sink, then return the fish and sweet potato back to the pan, add the paprika, lime juice, chives, salt and pepper and the beaten egg, then mash.

Take some fish cake mixture and squidge it into a fish-cake shape – this mixture should make 4–6, but it depends on the size you want them.

For the coating, put the lightly beaten egg in one bowl and the breadcrumbs in another. Dip a fish cake into the egg, spooning the egg all over and turning it around so that the fish cake is completely covered, then dip it in the breadcrumbs. Repeat with the other fish cakes. If you are going to shallow-fry them, they will hold their shape better in the pan if they are left in the fridge for an hour or so beforehand. Not essential, but good if you have the time. If you are baking them, they can go straight on a very lightly oiled baking tray and be baked straightaway in the oven for 20–30 minutes.

Serve the fish cakes in a large bap with loads of lettuce and mayonnaise and accompanied by lime quarters and a good glass of wine.

My dad's really very good lasagne

Involved? Yes, a little, but in the easiest of ways and all the ingredients are usually available from the local 'mini' supermarket, which I always find is a bonus. There is a little bit of chopping and browning and then the wonderful béchamel sauce needs to be made. When I used to go round to my dad's on the weekend, he would serve up this spectacular dish with some crusty garlic bread. Serves 6

150ml Madeira, red wine or stock (If you don't want to use the Madeira or wine, replace it with stock so you use 300ml stock in total)

100g pancetta chunks

1 red onion, peeled and finely chopped

2 large sprigs of fresh rosemary, finely chopped

2 tsp dried oregano

Oil, for cooking (optional)

2 cloves of garlic

500g lean beef mince

200g good-quality pork and leek or any really good sausage, skins removed

1 bay leaf

150ml good beef stock

1 x 400g tin of chopped tomatoes

3–4 large squidges of tomato purée

1 tsp sugar, preferably soft light brown (optional)

Salt and freshly ground black pepper

1 good bunch of fresh basil

Pour the Madeira or wine, if using, into a pan, bring to the boil and boil until the liquid has reduced by half. Keep an eye on it, as it does tend to reduce to nothing really quickly.

Meanwhile, in another pan, add the pancetta and cook until it is beginning to turn golden brown, then add the onion, rosemary and oregano and a little bit of oil, if needed, and cook until the onions are soft, about 10 minutes. Add the garlic and cook for a minute or so, then add the beef and pork along with the bay leaf. Use a wooden spoon to break up the meat and stir from time to time.

While the meat is cooking, pour the beef stock into the pan containing the reduced Madeira or wine. Bring to the boil and boil like mad until it is reduced by half. If you are just using stock, boil it until it is reduced to about a third of its original quantity. Again, this can happen quickly, so check it every minute. Once it is reduced, take the pan off the heat and set aside.

Once the meat has turned from pink to brown add the reduced wine/stock mix, the tin of tomatoes plus the juice, the tomato purée, sugar and some seasoning and stir together. Leave to simmer for about 15 minutes. Once cooked, there should be some liquid left in the meat, but it should not look too soupy.

My dad's really very good lasagne (continued)

8–10 lasagne sheets (no-need-to-precook type)

50g piece of Parmesan cheese

Béchamel sauce

40g butter, plus extra for greasing

40g flour

300ml double cream

300ml milk

Few good pinches of freshly grated nutmeg

Equipment

Medium lasagne dish, 30cm x 20cm

Meanwhile, make the béchamel sauce. Put the butter in a pan over a medium heat and heat until it melts, then take the pan off the heat and add the flour. Put the cream and milk together in a jug and add a little of it to the butter and flour. Using a wooden spoon, mix it together, then add a little more liquid and mix well, making sure that you get the wooden spoon into the edges of the pan to dislodge any of the flour/butter mix, which may be caught there. Keep adding the milk/cream mixture slowly, bit by bit, stirring well between each addition. Once all the cream mixture has been added, return the pan to the heat and bring it to the boil, stirring all the time. After a minute or so, the mixture will thicken slightly, then remove it from the heat, season well with a few good pinches of nutmeg and some salt and pepper and set aside.

By now the meat should be ready and the assembly can begin. Grease a lasagne dish with some butter, then spread a thin layer of the meat sauce on the bottom of the dish. Sprinkle over some basil leaves, then add a layer of lasagne sheets over the top, slightly overlapping to make sure that there are no gaps. Then spread another a layer of the meat sauce over the top, sprinkle over some more basil leaves and then some of the white sauce. Add another layer of pasta followed by the meat sauce and basil, then finish off with the white sauce. Grate some Parmesan on top and cook in the oven for 45 minutes.

Take the lasagne out of the oven, leave to cool for a few minutes and serve. This dish is even better on the second day when the flavours have had a chance to develop. Serve with a fine Italian red wine.

Heart-warming 'boeuf bourguignon' (with a touch of something Italian)

I regularly make stews for dinner, and there is something very comforting about this rich beef dish, teeming with deep and intense flavours. The dish tastes even better the day after it is made. Boeuf bourguignon purists will not be too pleased when they see the addition of the Italian wine Marsala to this traditional French dish. However, I find it makes the sauce more flavourful – mixing a little bit of French and a little bit of Italian creates a delicious partnership. Serves 4

Oil, for cooking

1kg braising steak, cut into large chunks

Salt and freshly ground black pepper

Glug of wine

200g bacon lardons

Handful of plain flour

1 clove of garlic, peeled and ground to a paste or finely chopped

2 sprigs of fresh rosemary

2 sprigs of fresh thyme

300ml Burgundy wine and 350ml Marsala or any other wine or 600–750ml very good beef stock

10–20 shallots, peeled (depending on their size)

1 medium carrot, peeled and sliced

Large handful of dried porcini mushrooms

Preheat the oven to 150°C (300°F), Gas Mark 3. Heat the oil in a large non-stick frying pan or sauté pan. Season the meat really well with salt and pepper, then add about a quarter of the meat to the pan and brown it well on all sides. Tip the meat into the casserole dish. If there are lots of brown and crusty bits in the pan, tip off the excess oil between batches, let it cool down a little and add glug of wine. Use a wooden spoon to scrape off the brown bits and tip them in the pan with the meat. Repeat with the rest of the meat, adding more oil if you need to.

Add half of the bacon to the pan and brown it well, then tip it into the casserole dish and repeat with the remaining bacon.

Season the flour with salt and pepper, then sprinkle it over the bacon and beef so that it is lightly covered and mix together so the flour is completely dissolved. Add the garlic, rosemary, thyme and a little salt (the lardons are quite salty) and pepper. Add just enough Burgundy and Marsala or stock to almost cover all the meat. Cover with a lid and cook in the oven for 2½ hours.

Meanwhile, heat some oil in the same frying pan you used for the meat, add the shallots and fry until they are turning a deep golden brown. Add the carrot and cook for a further minute, then set aside.

▶

Heart-warming 'boeuf bourguignon' (with a touch of something Italian)
(continued)

Equipment
Large casserole dish

After 2½ hours, carefully remove the meat from the oven and add the onion, carrots and porcini mushrooms, then return the casserole dish to the oven and cook for another 30 minutes. Once the bourguignon is ready, remove the dish from the oven. If there is still lots of liquid, remove the meat and vegetables from the mixture and boil the liquid over a high heat on the hob to reduce it a little, then return the meat and vegetables to the casserole dish.

Serve with some creamy mashed potatoes and a large glass of Burgundy.

Not-so-Cornish pasties with sturdy shortcrust pastry

I went to school in Devon, where pasties abound. I would love to tell you a story of me rushing down to the bakery to buy a hot Cornish pasty and eating it on the seafront with the wind rushing through my afro, but back then during my teen years a fast-food burger was my first Saturday afternoon love. It wasn't until I became an adult that I began to favour a good pasty for lunch, served hot from the baker or, better still, homemade.

Our beloved pasty has now been given special protected EU status. The only way a pasty can indeed be called Cornish is if it is made (but not necessarily baked) in Cornwall, follows a traditional recipe and is D-shaped and lies flat (never standing up). Here is my take on a proper Cornish pasty. Serves 4

Sturdy shortcrust

250g strong white bread flour, plus extra for dusting

250g plain flour

175g butter

5g salt

Up to 3 eggs

Water (optional)

Filling

200g minced beef

1 medium-sized potato, peeled and cut into small cubes

1 medium-sized onion, peeled and cut into small cubes

150g swede, peeled and cut into small cubes

1 clove of garlic, peeled and finely chopped

For the pastry, put the flour, butter and salt in a food processor and blitz to fine breadcrumbs. If you do not have a food processor, rub the flour and butter together using your fingertips to fine breadcrumbs. Add the eggs, one by one, blitzing if using the food processor or stirring well with a knife between each addition until the dough comes together in a ball. If the dough does not come together after two eggs, then add a further egg. If the dough is still too dry, add a little cold water. If the dough looks greasy and shiny at this point, shape it into a rough ball and place it in the fridge for 15 minutes or the freezer for about 7 minutes to allow the butter to firm up a little.

Preheat the oven to 200°C (400°F), Gas Mark 6. Once the dough is ready, roll it out on a floured surface to just over 5mm thick and cut out four 18cm-diameter circles. The easiest way to do this is to put a pan lid down on the pastry and cut around it with a knife, or just cut out an 18cm circle using greaseproof paper and use that as a template instead. When I make these, I usually get about three circles from the first rolling out. If the pastry is soft and greasy, just pop it in the fridge or freezer for a few minutes to become firmer.

▶

Not-so-Cornish pasties with sturdy shortcrust pastry
(continued)

- Small handful of fresh thyme or 1½ tbsp dried thyme
- 2 sprigs of fresh rosemary, finely chopped
- Few shakes of Worcestershire sauce
- Salt and freshly ground black pepper
- 50g butter
- 1 egg, lightly beaten

Put all of the filling ingredients, except the butter and beaten egg, together in a bowl and season very well. Lay out one of the pastry rounds and put a dollop of the meat and vegetable mix in the centre – the pasty should be nice and full but not bursting. Put a blob of the butter on top of the meat and vegetable mixture and brush around the outside of the circle with a little beaten egg. Fold the circle in half like a book and pinch to seal the edges together. There are two options, depending on how you like to eat yours. Will you be doing the much-loved flat D-shape or will you favour a stegosaurus-style pasty which stands upright, loud and proud? Starting at one end of the pasty, take the corner and fold a 1cm piece down, the way you would if you were folding down a corner in a book to mark the page, then take the very edge of that folded-down 'corner' – just the last 2mm of it – and fold that bit down as well. Keep pressing and folding this way until you reach the end of the sealed bit of the pastry.

Now place the pasty on a baking tray and repeat with the remaining pastry rounds and filling. Brush all the pasties over with more beaten egg and bake in the oven for about 30–40 minutes, or until a skewer inserted into the thickest part of the pasty comes out piping hot. Remove from the oven and serve straightaway.

Mum's chilli con carne

My mum used to work nights as a nurse, so she didn't have much time to cook, but now and again when she had some time off she would cook my brother and I the most fabulous chilli con carne, steaming hot with bags of flavour, and it would always taste better the second day. I have taken a bit of artistic licence here and added a couple of extra ingredients, but the comforting, warming flavour still remains the same. Serves 4

Oil, for cooking

1 large onion, peeled and chopped

1 clove of garlic, peeled and chopped

2 tsp soft light brown sugar

1 bay leaf

1 tsp dried oregano

1 tsp paprika or cayenne pepper

1 tsp ground cumin

1 tsp chilli powder (or to taste)

1 red pepper, deseeded and chopped

1 red chilli, deseeded and finely chopped (optional)

500g minced beef

1 small glug of a good red wine (optional)

2 x 400g tins of cherry tomatoes (plum will work well too)

Few glugs of Worcestershire sauce

1 x 400g tin of kidney beans, drained and rinsed

Salt and freshly ground black pepper

Heat the oil in a pan over a medium heat, add the onion and cook for about 10 minutes, or until it is nice and soft. Add the garlic and cook for 1 minute, then stir in the brown sugar, bay leaf, oregano and paprika or cayenne, cumin, chilli powder, red pepper, chilli and minced beef. Use a wooden spoon to break up any large bits of meat, turn up the heat and keep stirring so it does not burn on the bottom on the pan, for about 5 minutes. Once the meat has turned brown, I sometimes add a glug of red wine and boil it for 2 minutes to get rid of the strong alcoholic taste, but if you don't fancy using any alcohol, just skip this stage.

Now add the cherry tomatoes, Worcestershire sauce, kidney beans and a good amount of salt and pepper. Bring to the boil, then reduce the heat and leave to simmer for an hour or so, stirring it from time to time to prevent the mixture sticking to the bottom of the pan. Check the mixture after 30 minutes and, if most of the liquid has evaporated, add a little water or stock, then stir and leave to simmer away and develop all the lovely flavours.

Serve with some soft white rice and topped with some coriander leaves. Or try serving the chilli with some tortilla crips, soured cream, guacamole and some salsa.

Lamb, chickpea & pear tagine

This tagine sounds weird but it tastes wonderful, as it packs a massive punch. Not the shortest ingredients list in the world, but I find the extra little bit of shopping oh-so-worth it. I have made this tagine a few times when my family and friends have come over for a meal – a really great dish for entertaining. Serves 6

- Oil, for cooking
- 100g plain flour
- Salt and freshly ground black pepper
- 700–750g diced lamb
- 1 large onion, peeled and chopped into chunks
- 3 cloves of garlic, peeled and squashed
- 1 tsp ground cinnamon
- 1 tsp ground ginger
- 1 tsp ground allspice
- 1 tsp garam masala (not strictly a North African ingredient but very tasty nonetheless)
- Few juniper berries (optional)
- 1 x 400g tin of tomatoes plus the juice
- 450ml good lamb, beef or chicken stock
- 3 pears, peeled, deseeded and quartered
- I x 400g tin of chickpeas, drained
- 1 bunch of fresh coriander leaves, roughly chopped

Heat the oil in a large pan. Put the flour on a large plate and season with salt and pepper. Add the lamb and toss until coated, then add the lamb to the pan and cook over a high heat for about 3 minutes, stirring frequently. Add the onion, garlic, cinnamon, ginger, allspice, garam masala and juniper berries, if using, along with a good amount of salt and pepper and cook for 5 minutes or so, stirring frequently to make sure it doesn't burn.

Now add the tin of tomatoes and stock, bring to a gentle simmer and leave to simmer for about 1 hour. At this stage the lamb should be almost ready. Add the pears and chickpeas and cook for a further 15 minutes, or until the lamb is lovely and tender. I usually find the sauce just the right thickness at this stage, but if the lamb is cooked and there is too much sauce, strain it through a large sieve set over a bowl. Keep the lamb warm and pour the sauce back into the pan, bring to the boil and boil until it has thickened. If there is not enough sauce, add a little water or stock.

Taste and adjust the seasoning, adding more salt or pepper if you like. Sprinkle over the coriander leaves and serve with some fluffy couscous that has been cooked in stock and sprinkled with some toasted pine nuts. Some supermarkets actually sell toasted pine nuts ready to go, which is a real bonus! Serve with a hot pot of Moroccan mint tea.

Chicken Paillard with herbed warm butter & crushed new potatoes

I first had this dish in a restaurant a couple of years ago and totally fell in love with it. It is a classic French dish, which is so quick and easy to cook, and makes a regular appearance in my house, served piping hot with a lovely glass of white wine. Serves 4

- 500g small new potatoes
- Handful of chopped fresh parsley
- Handful of fresh thyme leaves or 1 tbsp dried thyme
- Handful of fresh oregano, finely chopped or 1 tbsp dried oregano
- Salt and freshly ground black pepper
- 4 chicken breasts
- Oil, for cooking
- Grated zest and juice of 1 lemon
- 75g butter, plus an extra 50g for the potatoes

Cook the potatoes in a large pan of boiling water, then drain and return them to the pan. Cover with a lid and keep warm.

Meanwhile, divide the herbs into 4 small piles. Season a chopping board (one you don't mind using for meat) with salt and pepper, then sprinkle a half of one of the piles of herbs over the centre of the chopping board. Put the chicken on top and sprinkle with the other half of the pile of herbs together with some more salt and pepper. Place a large piece of clingfilm over the top, and, using a rolling pin, bash the chicken breast so that it is about 5mm thick all over. Peel off the clingfilm (saving it) and set the chicken breast aside. Repeat with the other three chicken breasts.

Heat some oil in a frying pan, and when the pan is hot add two chicken breasts. Sprinkle over some lemon zest and a squeeze of lemon and fry for about 2–3 minutes on each side, or until the chicken is cooked. To check that the chicken is done, insert a knife into the thickest part of one and press slightly, the juices should run clear. When the chicken is almost ready, add half of the 75g of butter to the pan, tilt the pan slightly and use a small teaspoon to spoon the butter over the chicken breasts. Remove from the pan and repeat with the other two chicken breasts.

Crush the cooked and drained potatoes slightly, then add the remaining 50g butter and some salt and pepper and serve with the chicken and a large green salad.

Minted lamb & coriander burgers with cucumber yoghurt

Make a double batch of these burgers and freeze the ones you don't use. These are great in the summer for barbecues and also in the winter for cosy evenings in. Serves 4

450g minced lamb

1 large onion, peeled, roughly grated and squeezed of excess liquid

1 small garlic clove, peeled and finely chopped

Small handful of raisins (about 25g), roughly chopped

2 tsp ground cumin

2 tsp ground coriander

1 tsp ground cinnamon

Small handful of fresh mint leaves, finely chopped

Small handful of fresh coriander leaves, finely chopped

1 egg

Handful of dried breadcrumbs (about 50g)

Sea salt and freshly ground black pepper

2 tbsp sunflower oil

4 sesame baps, toasted, to serve

Cucumber yoghurt

10cm piece of cucumber

150g Greek yoghurt (low fat if you are feeling righteous)

Small handful of fresh mint leaves, finely chopped

Preheat the oven to 200°C (400°F), Gas Mark 6. Put all the burger ingredients, except the oil and baps, in a large bowl with salt and pepper and squish everything together well until evenly mixed. Divide the mixture into four even-sized pieces and shape each one into a 2.5cm-thick burger.

Heat the oil in a large ovenproof frying pan over a medium heat and cook the burgers for 2–3 minutes on each side until well browned. Then place them in the oven for 10–12 minutes or so until the burgers are piping hot and cooked in the middle.

Meanwhile, prepare the yoghurt. Peel the cucumber and cut it in half along its length. Remove the seeds with a small spoon and finely chop the remaining flesh, then put it into a medium bowl and mix with the yoghurt, mint and enough seasoning to taste.

Serve the burgers in the toasted sesame baps with a dollop of the cucumber yoghurt.

Paprika baked fish with chorizo, lemon & thyme

Chorizo with thyme is one of my favourite combinations and it goes well with chicken, fish and even bread. Spice up some white fish with this powerful rainbow of tastes.

Serves 4

175g chorizo, cut into chunks

Handful of chopped fresh thyme

4 white fish fillets, like haddock, cod or pollack (preferably sustainably caught), skinned

Salt and freshly ground black pepper

2 pinches of paprika, or to taste

Grated zest of 1 lemon (the rest of the lemon can be quartered and used as a garnish)

1 tbsp olive oil

10–12 cherry tomatoes

5–10 cloves of garlic, peeled

Preheat the oven to 200°C (400°F), Gas Mark 6. Put the chorizo and thyme in a frying pan and cook over a high heat for about 5 minutes then set aside.

Put the fish in a roasting tin, season with salt, pepper and paprika and sprinkle over some of the lemon zest. Drizzle over the olive oil and sprinkle the tomatoes and the garlic around. Tip two-thirds of the chorizo mix over the fish and bake in the oven for 8–10 minutes.

Remove the fish from the oven and sprinkle over the rest of the chorizo and the lemon zest. Return to the oven and cook for a further 5 minutes, or until the fish is opaque and shiny inside. Serve immediately with crunchy sautéed potatoes or oven-baked chips and a crunchy green salad.

Rioja-braised lamb shanks with chorizo & garlic

I have tried so many different combinations with lamb shanks and it is such a wonderful joint of meat, so any excuse to be able to cook it over and over again is fine by me. I have a secret love affair with Barcelona. The first time I went there, I fell in love with the place, especially with the food. Potatoes in tomato sauce, fine Spanish wines and sizzling plates of prawns and chorizo, so I took some of my favourite Spanish ingredients and put them together to make this dish. Once the initial faff of browning the meat is done, this dish requires very little effort and the flavours are intense. Serves 4

- 4 lamb shanks
- Salt and freshly ground black pepper
- Oil, for cooking
- 350ml Rioja or 350ml good-quality beef stock
- 250ml good-quality balsamic vinegar (if using the less expensive stuff just use 100ml balsamic, plus 150ml stock or Rioja)
- 1 whole bulb of garlic, cut in half horizontally
- 2 bay leaves
- 1–2 tsp paprika (or to taste)
- Few black peppercorns
- 4 sprigs of fresh rosemary
- 300ml beef stock
- 125g chorizo (one long skinny sausage, rather than slices)
- 1 large red onion, peeled and cut into wedges
- 2 carrots, peeled and chopped
- 1 squidge of honey, to taste (optional)

Preheat the oven to 150°C (300°F), Gas Mark 3. Season the lamb well with salt and pepper, add a little oil to the pan and heat over a high heat. Turn down the heat slightly and brown the lamb shanks all over, then transfer them to a large pan. I find it easier using two frying pans, putting two lamb shanks in each and browning them at the same time.

Pour the wine and balsamic vinegar into the pan and boil for 5 minutes, then add the lamb shanks, garlic, bay leaves, paprika, peppercorns, half the rosemary and stock. Place the pan over a high heat, cover with a lid and bring it to the boil. As soon as it is boiling, take the pan off the heat, place it in the oven and cook for 2 hours.

Remove the pan from the oven and add the chorizo, onion, carrots, honey to taste, if using, and the rest of the rosemary, then return to the oven and cook for another hour, or until the meat is almost falling off the bone and you can pull the meat away from the bone with little effort.

Scoop the meat and vegetables out of the pan with a slotted spoon and keep warm. I leave a few garlic cloves in to intensify the flavours. If you would like the sauce to be thicker, put the pan back on the heat and bring to the boil. I like to boil it like mad for about 8–10 minutes until it is the right thickness, then leave to cool slightly. Taste and adjust the seasoning if necessary.

Serve the meat and vegetables with smooth creamy mashed potatoes and lashings of the lamb shank sauce.

Pan-fried balsamic pear salad with pancetta, Gorgonzola & a warm honey dressing

I just love a good salad. When it is cold outside, having a substantial salad with a warm dressing really is just the ticket. Serves 4

2 x 120g bag of rocket leaves

16 slices of pancetta

2 knobs of butter

Oil, for cooking

4 pears, peeled, deseeded, cored and quartered

Salt and freshly ground black pepper

1 squidge of honey, plus extra squidges for the dressing

A couple of drizzles of balsamic vinegar, plus 2 tbsp for the dressing

1 blob of Dijon mustard

Good handful of pine nuts, toasted (I found some pre-toasted at the supermarket; or pan-fry them for 3 minutes, or until toasted)

150g Gorgonzola cheese, ripped into chunks

Distribute the rocket evenly among four serving plates.

Put the pancetta in a frying pan over a medium–high heat and cook until really crispy, then remove from the pan and leave to drain on some kitchen paper.

Put the butter and oil in a frying pan over a low heat. Once the butter has melted, place the pears in the pan with some salt and pepper and one squidge of honey. Turn up the heat and cook for about 5 minutes. Add a good drizzle of vinegar and cook for another minute, then take the pan off the heat. Remove the pears from the pan, reserving any juice that may be left in there.

Arrange the pears and pancetta on top of the rocket leaves so each person has four quarters each. Now put the pan back on the heat and add the remaining knob of butter, a few squidges of honey, the mustard, salt and pepper and the pine nuts and cook briefly until the sauce is heated through.

Pour the sauce over the pears and the rocket, then scatter the ripped-up Gorgonzola on top and serve.

Hearty Spanish paella with sherry, chorizo & prawns

I am a massive fan of Spain: the food, the culture and the people. I first had paella on a trip with my dad to Alicante and loved it. Ideally this needs to be cooked in a large wide pan that can fit the rice in a single layer, but any large frying pan will do. I have used Arborio rice, but paella rice is great if you can find it or even basmati. In fact, I once started to make this dish and realised I did not have enough Arborio rice, so I used 200g of Arborio and 100g of basmati and the dish worked a treat! Serves 6

1–2 tbsp oil, plus extra for cooking the paella

Salt and freshly ground black pepper

2 skinless, boneless chicken breasts, cut into very large chunks

150g chorizo, in large chunks

2 cloves of garlic, peeled and chopped

2 pinches of paprika (or to taste)

150ml Oloroso sherry, optional (or make up this amount with stock)

300g Arborio rice

Pinch of saffron (optional)

Knob of butter

400ml chicken stock

1 large bunch of spring onions, trimmed and sliced

250g raw prawns, unpeeled

150g frozen peas

1 bunch of fresh flat-leaf parsley leaves, finely chopped

Lime wedges, to serve

Heat the oil in a large sauté pan or frying pan. Season the chicken pieces, add to the pan and brown them well all over, adding more oil if necessary. Add the chorizo and fry for a further minute. Throw in the garlic and cook for a couple of minutes, then add the paprika. Take the pan off the heat to cool a little, then add half the sherry, if using.

Return the pan to the heat and bring to the boil. Boil for a couple of minutes to drive off the strong alcoholic taste, then add the rice, saffron, butter and stock. Turn the heat down and leave to simmer for 30 minutes or so until most of the liquid has been soaked up by the rice. Don't mix the rice, as it will get that lovely crunchy layer on the bottom. Halfway through the cooking time, put the lid on the pan. If you are using a pan that does not have a lid, just place a flat baking tray over the top.

Once the rice is cooked, take the pan off the heat. In another frying pan, or pan, heat a little oil over a high heat, then add the spring onions and fry for a couple of minutes until they start to turn golden. Add the prawns and cook until they are piping hot, then add the frozen peas and cook until they are defrosted. Take the pan off the heat for a minute or so to cool down. If you are using sherry, add the remaining sherry to the prawn mix and boil for a minute or so, then tip the contents of the pan into the rice and chicken mixture. If you are not using sherry, just tip the prawn mixture into the rice. Return the rice pan to the heat and cook for a minute or so until piping hot.

Divide the paella among serving plates, sprinkle over the parsley and serve with lime wedges.

Mini beef Wellingtons with morel mushrooms, sherry & thyme

As always, the sherry in this dish is optional. I made this recipe for a very small family gathering, telling everyone ahead of the day what foods were on the menu. Everyone was totally into it except one person, who shall remain nameless, who said that they would like theirs with no pastry. And so, the 'naked' beef Wellington was born – although I prefer to eat my Wellingtons fully clad! Serves 4

1 x 500g packet of puff pastry

Plain flour, for dusting

1 x 20g packet of dried jumbo morels or 20g dried porcini mushrooms

Oil, for cooking

Salt and freshly ground black pepper

4 x 180g slices of beef fillet

4 small shallots, peeled and very finely chopped

Knob of butter

500g chestnut mushrooms, wiped and finely chopped

1 generous glug of medium sweet sherry (optional)

Large handful of fresh thyme leaves

1 egg, lightly beaten, for the eggwash

300ml double cream

Roll out the puff pastry on a well-floured work surface to 0.5cm and about 36 x 36cm square. Trim the edges with a sharp knife to neaten them up a little if necessary, then cut the square into four squares and place them on two baking trays. Pop them in the fridge for 5 minutes to firm up a little.

Rinse the dried mushrooms in cold water, then put them in a small bowl and cover with hot water. Leave to soak for 20 minutes.

Meanwhile, heat some oil in a frying pan and heat until very hot. Season the beef well all over and pan-fry it for 1 minute on each side, then set aside.

Put the shallots in the pan and fry for 4–5 minutes or so until softened, then add the butter and chestnut mushrooms and cook for a few minutes.

Meanwhile, drain the morels (save the liquid for a soup or stock) and finely chop, then add them to the pan together with the glug of sherry, if using. Turn up the heat and cook until most of the sherry has evaporated and the mushrooms are looking dryish and not too mushy. Add the thyme, check the seasoning and cook for 1 more minute, then take the pan off the heat and set aside.

Mini beef Wellingtons with morel mushrooms, sherry & thyme
(continued)

Preheat the oven to 200°C (400°F), Gas Mark 6. Remove the pastry from the fridge – it should be maleable but not too soft. Put a large tablespoon of the mushroom mixture into the centre of the pastry and spread it out to the same size as a beef steak. Pop the steak on top and brush a little of the eggwash around the edges of the pastry. Draw up the corners and edges of the pastry so they meet and overlap slightly in the middle. Turn it right side up and shape it round the sides a little with your hands. Repeat with the other three beef fillets and pastry squares. There will be a good amount of mushroom mixture left over, and this is for the sauce later. If the pastry is too soft, put it in the fridge for 5 minutes or so to firm up. This will make sure the pastry does not just melt into a gooey mess in the oven before it has had a chance to puff up. Before baking, slash the tops to a design of your liking and brush them all over with more eggwash. Cook in the oven for about 14 minutes for medium rare, or cook for longer or shorter depending on how you like your beef.

Five minutes before the Wellingtons are ready, reheat the mushroom mixture. When it is hot, add the double cream and cook on a high heat for 2 minutes. Taste and adjust the seasoning if necessary, then take off the heat and cover with a lid to keep warm.

When the Wellingtons are ready, remove them from the oven and serve with the sauce and a big glass of a hearty red wine.

Prawn bisque with basil & brandy

This dish requires a little effort and good large prawns are often not cheap, but it is definitely worth making. One freezing cold winter's day, a good friend of mine organised a lunch date over in Shoreditch. Over lunch I had some of the finest food I have had in a long time, I met a fabulous chef called Pierre Koffman and his lovely wife Claire. Pierre is one of the godfathers of the chef world, having had the likes of Marco Pierre White and Gordon Ramsay through his kitchens. I found one of his old books and after reading it, I was inspired to write this recipe, so Pierre and Claire, this one is for you. Serves 4 as a starter

1 large red onion, peeled and finely chopped

Oil, for cooking

15–20 large raw prawns

1 clove of garlic

1 bay leaf

2–3 very big squirts of tomato purée

125ml brandy

650ml good-quality fish or vegetable stock

60ml double cream

1 carrot, peeled and roughly chopped

Paprika, to taste

2 knobs of butter, plus an extra knob if necessary

Salt and freshly ground black pepper

1 heaped tbsp plain flour, plus extra if necessary

½ bunch of fresh basil, leaves only

Put the onion in a medium pan with some oil and cook over a very low heat for about 10 minutes.

Meanwhile, remove the shells and tails from the prawns and set aside. As soon as the onions are soft, put the shells and tails in the pan and cook, stirring from time to time, over a high heat for about 2–3 minutes, or until the prawn shells have turned pink. Add the garlic, bay leaf and tomato purée and cook for 1 minute, then add 75ml of the brandy. If the brandy does not evaporate in one go, turn up the heat and let it boil for a minute or so. Now pour in the stock, cream, carrot and paprika. Bring to the boil, then turn down the heat and leave to simmer for 30 minutes.

Five minutes before the stock is ready, melt a knob of butter in a frying pan over a medium–high heat. As soon as the butter is sizzling, add the prawns and salt and pepper and cook for 2–3 minutes. Add the remaining 50ml brandy and cook for another minute to get rid of the strong alcoholic taste, then take the pan off the heat.

Put a sieve over a bowl and pour in the stock mixture. Using the end of a rolling pin or a potato masher, squish the shells so that all the flavour is squeezed out through the sieve. It's important to spend a good 5 minutes on this because this is where all the flavour lives. Discard the shells, reserving the stock.

Prawn bisque with basil & brandy (continued)

Rinse out the pan in which you cooked the prawn stock, add the other knob of butter and the flour and stir gently together to form a paste. Gradually add the prawn stock, stirring all the time to avoid any lumps. Once you have added all the stock, increase the heat and boil it like mad for a minute or so until it has thickened. If you would like the bisque a little thinner, add a splash more water. If you would like it thicker, put another small knob of butter into a mug, add a tablespoon of flour and a few tablespoons of the stock and mix to combine, then add the mixture to the bisque and boil again for 1 minute.

Now pop the prawns and any liquid left in the frying pan into the pan with the stock, and heat through for 30 seconds or so.

Divide the bisque among four bowls and sprinkle with some basil leaves. Serve with some warm crusty bread. This soup is rather filling and quite possibly one of the tastiest things I have ever eaten.

Twice-cooked chicken Kiev

This is a classic, but a delicious one at that. The first couple of times I made this dish, the butter leaked out because I was a bit rough with it. Once I learned how to handle the chicken with care, the dish was a resounding success. It is a lovely dinner party dish and handy, too, as the chicken can be prepared ahead of time and cooked once the guests have arrived. Serves 4

4 chicken breasts, about 175g each

100g garlic and parsley butter (see page 238), well chilled

75g plain flour

4 medium eggs, lightly beaten

150g dried breadcrumbs, like Japanese Panko crumbs

Sea salt and freshly ground black pepper

About 600ml sunflower oil

Lemon wedges, to serve

Lay a chicken breast smooth side down on a sheet of baking parchment. Lay another piece of baking parchment on top and, using a meat mallet or rolling pin, bash the chicken fairly thinly to about 5mm in thickness. It should be thin enough to wrap easily around the butter but not so thin as to break up or become see-through. Repeat with the remaining three breasts.

Divide the garlic and parsley butter into four finger-length pieces. If you have to reshape the butter as it has become quite soft, refrigerate it until it has hardened into its new shape.

Lay a flattened chicken breast out with the length running away from you, season and then put a finger of butter near the end closest to you, running from left to right across the breast. Pick up the edge of the chicken closest to you and begin to roll it over the butter while at the same time flipping the left and right sides of the chicken inwards. Continue to roll the chicken away from you, making sure the edges remain tucked in as you go. You should have a perfect little chicken parcel when you reach the end. Repeat with the remaining chicken and butter.

Put the flour in a large shallow bowl, the eggs in another bowl and the dried breadcrumbs in another. Season each one with a little salt and pepper. You can also add some dried herbs like oregano, or thyme or chopped fresh herbs, if you like.

Twice-cooked chicken Kiev
(continued)

Carefully dip the chicken parcels in the flour first, making sure they are well covered and shaking off any excess (this will help the egg to stick), then dip them in the egg and finally in the breadcrumbs, making sure they are well covered. Repeat this process again, in the same order – flour, eggs and breadcrumbs. Place the coated chicken breasts in the fridge for 30 minutes or so until the coating is firm.

Preheat the oven to 180°C (350°F), Gas Mark 4. About 5 minutes before you are ready to cook the chicken, heat the oil in a wide sauté pan until a small cube of white bread dropped into the oil browns in 30–60 seconds. Remove the chicken breasts from the fridge and very carefully place two of them into the hot oil for about 30 seconds–1 minute until crisp and golden brown. Carefully remove them with a slotted spoon and drain on kitchen paper, then transfer them to a baking tray. Repeat with the remaining two breasts. Next, bake them in the oven for about 15 minutes, or until the chicken is cooked.

Remove the chicken from the oven and serve immediately. This dish is quite rich, so serve with some lemon wedges and a fresh, crisp mixed green salad.

Not-so-slow roast leg of lamb with thyme & plum gravy

So I tried it – the seven-hour roast leg of lamb. I put the lamb in the oven early afternoon, then I cleaned the house, answered emails, did the ironing and, my goodness, I also baked a cake. And yet after that, four hours still remained. Finally, all bleary eyed, shortly after dark and when the rest of the family had filled up on other foods through hunger and lack of patience, I pulled the joint out the oven. Admittedly it was divine – dark, soft and so very flavourful, but to have something tantalising me in the oven for that long and not being able to taste it is something I simply cannot bear. The longest I can wait is six hours for my slow-roast pork shoulder! I decided to bring the dish into the 21st century and make it into something I would cook again and again, so I developed this shortcut version, which is ready in under a couple of hours and never ceases to please. Serves 4–5

- 1 x 2kg whole leg of lamb (bone still in)
- Oil, for rubbing
- Sea salt and freshly ground black pepper
- 1 bulb of garlic, cloves separated, papery skins removed and each clove cut in half
- 1 large bunch of fresh thyme
- Few anchovies or Worcestershire sauce

Red wine and plum gravy

- 1 good glass of an equally good red wine (the better the wine, the better the gravy)
- 1 tbsp plain flour
- 550ml good-quality liquid stock
- 1 dollop of plum jam

Preheat the oven to 250°C (500°F), Gas Mark 10. Massage the lamb with some oil and place it on a wire rack or trivet in the roasting tin. Season the meat all over with salt and pepper, then use a small sharp knife to make incisions in the flesh. Push a bit of the garlic and some thyme in each slot, making sure they are pushed well in so they don't burn in the oven. Push some anchovies into some of the slots as well, if using, or sprinkle Worcestershire sauce over the meat. I know not everyone likes anchovies, but once cooked they give meat a wonderful flavour without actually tasting like anchovies.

Put the lamb in the oven for 20 minutes until brown, then turn the oven temperature down to 160°C (315°F), Gas Mark 2–3 and cook the meat for about 1 hour and 10 minutes.

Once the lamb is cooked, remove it from the oven and put it in another tin, keeping all the liquid from the roasting for the gravy. Turn the oven off, put the meat back in, open the oven door and leave the lamb for 30 minutes to rest. Alternatively, remove the lamb from the oven, put on a warmed plate and cover with foil.

►

Not-so-slow roast leg of lamb with thyme & plum gravy (continued)

Equipment

Large roasting tin with a wire rack or trivet placed in the tin

While the lamb is resting, make the gravy. Pour off as much of the fat as possible from the roasting tin, then put the tin on the hob, add the wine and bring to the boil over a high heat. Boil like mad until it is reduced by half, scraping off the bits from the bottom of the tin. Sprinkle the flour in one corner of the tin and mix it with a little of the reduced wine to remove any lumps, then add the stock and mix it with the flour mixture to combine.

Taste and adjust the seasoning. Add 1 tablespoon of the plum jam and heat through gently, stirring all the time. The gravy should begin to thicken slightly. Taste again, adjusting the seasoning if required, and serve with the gorgeous lamb. If there any lumps and bumps in the gravy, sieve them out, but I rather like the uneven textures. Serve with some deliciously crispy roasties and green vegetables.

Vegetables & Vegetarian

Some of these dishes are not strictly vegetarian, unless you use the many vegetarian cheese options out there. This chapter also comes full of different vegetable accompaniments to have with other meals. I am a potato lover – chipped, boiled or fried or any other way they come – and my Hasselback tatties are both a visual delight and a great way to jazz up your usual roasties. The baked mushroom, chestnut and pea risotto with truffle oil smells and tastes so good that it makes me smile, and the spinach, rocket and Parmesan roulade is a great make-ahead dish if you are entertaining. I was not a fan of broccoli until I stuck it in the oven one day and baked it – what a difference! Another revelation, sweet potato wedges baked with paprika and maple-glazed bacon makes great movie night, stay-at-home finger food for cold winter evenings.

'Cooking is like love, it should be entered into with wild abandon or not at all.'

Harriet van Horne

Gruyère & mustard cauliflower cheese

I ordered one of those organic veggie boxes earlier in the year and a whole feast of exciting fruit and vegetables landed on my doorstep at five in the morning. However, at the end of the week, when the mango, grapes and perfectly soft pears were all but a wonderful distant memory, the large creamy coloured cauliflower stared at me forlornly from the bottom of the fridge. I made cauliflower cheese with it, which I had not made in a long time and oh, my … cauliflower just became my new favourite veg. Serves 4–6

- 1 large cauliflower, stem and leaves removed, cut into small even-sized florets
- Oil, for drizzling
- 30g butter
- 30g plain flour
- Pinch of mustard powder
- 150ml milk
- 150ml single cream
- Pinch of cayenne pepper
- 60g blue cheese or mature Cheddar
- ½ bunch of finely chopped fresh chives
- Salt and freshly ground black pepper
- Large handful of dried breadcrumbs
- 30g Gruyère or Parmesan cheese (or use vegetarian Parmesan-style cheese)
- Pinch of freshly ground nutmeg

Preheat the oven to 220°C (425°F), Gas Mark 7. Put the cauliflower in a small roasting tin with a tiny drizzle of oil and cover well with foil. Put it into the oven while it is heating up for upto 20 minutes – keeping a close eye on it – it will cook a little and you can avoid having to boil it first.

Meanwhile, make the sauce. Put the butter in a small pan over a medium heat. Once it has melted, add the flour and cook for 1 minute, stirring from time to time, then add the mustard and take the pan off the heat. Pour the milk and cream into a jug and add it very slowly to the flour mixture. I usually add about a quarter, stir it like mad to get rid of any lumps, then add a little more and stir it well again. If the liquid is added too quickly, there will be lots of lumps. If it is becoming lumpy, use a whisk to beat it like mad, and the lumps should disappear. Keep on adding the milk, stirring well until you have a lovely smooth sauce.

Return the pan to a medium heat and cook the sauce for a minute or so, then turn up the heat and let it boil for 1–2 minutes, or until the sauce thickens. Take the pan off the heat and add the blue cheese and chives.

Take the cauliflower out of the oven and remove the foil. If any moisture has accumulated in the roasting tin, tip it out and pour the cheese sauce over the cauliflower. Season with a little pepper (it probably will not need any salt, as the cheese is quite salty). Sprinkle over the breadcrumbs and the grated Gruyère and sprinkle a little nutmeg on top. Put the cauliflower back into the oven and cook for about 20–25 minutes, or until the sauce is bubbling and golden brown.

Pan-fried asparagus with toasted flaked almonds

My mother used to toast almonds at Christmas and put them on the 'goodie tray' in the living room along with the other Yuletide sweets and chocolates. I have paired these nuts with asparagus here, which I think go together really well. The asparagus is pan-fried, which adds a pleasant chargrilled taste. Serve with meat, fish or add to a large green salad drizzled with balsamic vinegar and olive oil. Serves 3–4 *(V)*

- 3 knobs of butter
- 50g flaked almonds
- Oil, for cooking
- 400g asparagus spears, woody ends trimmed off
- Salt and freshly ground black pepper

Put a knob of butter into a frying pan, add the flaked almonds and cook for about a minute or two until the nuts are turning golden brown. Tip the almonds out onto some kitchen paper to drain.

Add another knob of butter and a little oil to the pan and heat over a medium–high heat until the oil is hot. Add the asparagus and cook for about 4–6 minutes, or until the asparagus is soft and tender but still has a bit of bite. Add the toasted flaked almonds and check the dish for seasoning, adding some salt and pepper if necessary. If there is enough butter in the pan, cook until the butter turns golden brown and smells nutty; if not, add another knob of butter and cook over a high heat until it begins to go brown. Once everything is ready, serve straightaway.

Hot buttered green beans with spring onions & pomegranate

It is tough to get certain members of the family to eat green beans in my house. Add spring onions and pomegranate, however, and I can't seem to make enough of them.

Serves 4 *(V)*

400g green beans, trimmed

Salt and freshly ground black pepper

Large knob of butter

Large bunch of spring onions, trimmed and finely sliced

Large handful of pomegranate seeds

Cook the green beans in a pan of boiling salted water for 3 minutes. Most people have a certain way they like their beans cooked; I like mine just tender but still bright green with lots of crunch.

Meanwhile, melt the butter in a pan over a medium–high heat, add the spring onions and cook for a minute, then set aside.

When the beans are ready, drain, then tip them into the frying pan with the onions and mix everything together. Add the pomegranate seeds, season well with pepper and a little salt and serve.

Tarragon, parsley & mint crushed buttered new potatoes

I think I have a mild addiction to this dish. There is nothing better than a plate of new potatoes absolutely slathered in butter and flavoured with herbs. This dish is not reinventing the wheel, but it is just so delicious that I wanted to share it with you. Serves 4 *(V)*

800g baby new potatoes, scrubbed

80g butter

Salt and freshly ground black pepper

Handful (in total) of fresh tarragon, parsley and mint, roughly chopped

Cook the potatoes in a large pan of boiling water until a knife slides through the centre of one of the bigger ones easily, about 12–15 minutes. Drain, then return the potatoes to the now-dry pan and place over a low heat. Add the butter, salt and pepper and, using a potato masher, very gently crush the potatoes. I like to keep them quite whole and just apply a little bit of pressure to break them up slightly. Stir gently so that the potatoes are covered with the butter and seasoning.

Sprinkle over the herbs and serve immediately.

Roast carrots with lemon & thyme

Carrots on their own are just about bearable, but carrots with lemon and thyme? This gives my favourite orange root vegetable a little something extra. Serves 4–6 *(V)*

1kg carrots, trimmed and peeled (use baby carrots or cut large carrots into finger-length pieces)

Sea salt and freshly ground black pepper

2 tbsp olive oil

Small handful of fresh thyme leaves

Grated zest of 1 lemon

Large knob of butter, softened

Preheat the oven to 200°C (400°F), Gas Mark 6. Cook the carrots in a pan of boiling salted water for 10 minutes, or until just cooked (they may still be a little bit hard at this stage, but that is okay). Drain the carrots well, tip them onto a large baking tray and shuffle them into a single layer. Drizzle the olive oil over and sprinkle with the thyme leaves and salt and pepper.

Roast the carrots in the oven for about 35 minutes, then scatter the lemon zest over and return to roast for a final 10 minutes until tender and catching on the edges. If the lemon zest goes in too early, it will taste bitter.

Take out of the oven, toss the knob of butter through and serve at once.

Red cabbage with pears & garlic

A great accompaniment to a pork or turkey roast, a large ham or some juicy fat sausages. You can use apples instead of the pears, if you like, but as you can see from this book, I have a huge food crush on pears – pan-fried, roasted or just served as they are. One of the great food sensations for me is biting into a perfectly ripe pear and then feeling its exquisite juice dribble down my chin. I digress; pears and cabbage are a classic combination that goes down very nicely thank you very much. Serves 5–6 *(V)*

Oil, for cooking

2 red onions, peeled and sliced

1 tsp allspice

Salt and freshly ground black pepper

80g soft light brown sugar

2 cloves of garlic, peeled and finely sliced

1 large red cabbage, outer leaves and stem removed, then sliced

60ml red wine vinegar or balsamic vinegar

2 pears, peeled, cored and cubed

Knob of butter

Equipment

Large ovenproof pan or casserole dish

Preheat the oven to 180°C (350°F), Gas Mark 4. Heat some oil in a large pan over a low–medium heat, add the onions and cook for about 10 minutes until they begin to soften. Add the allspice, salt and pepper, sugar and garlic and cook for a couple more minutes. Add the cabbage, and vinegar, then stir the mixture and bring just to the boil.

If the pan you are using is not ovenproof, tip the mixture into a casserole dish, cover with a tight-fitting lid or foil and cook in the oven for 1 hour, or until the cabbage is soft. Halfway through the cooking time, take the pan or dish out of the oven and stir everything round a few times, then add the pears. Return to the oven for the rest of the cooking time.

Once the cabbage is cooked, take the pan or dish out of the oven and stir in the butter. Check for seasoning and serve.

Paprika baked sweet potato wedges with honey-glazed bacon & herby crème fraîche

The sweet potato is a relatively new addition to my cooking collection. My first taste of sweet potato was when I was travelling around Australia in the early nineties. In a small café in Byron Bay on the East coast, my travelling companion ordered a plate of wafer-thin sweet potato chips, covered in Parmesan cheese. In danger of eating all of hers, I ordered myself a portion and quizzed the Italian chef about my new orange veggie find. Nowadays I like to eat them in wedges with lashings of paprika; the addition of honey-glazed bacon is just pure greed, but in the case of these deep ochre-coloured beauties, sometimes greed is good. Serves 4–5

About 6–8 medium sweet potatoes, unpeeled

Oil, for drizzling (you can use olive oil spray, if you like)

Salt and freshly ground black pepper

Paprika, to taste

Dollop of English mustard

Good glug of maple syrup

6 rashers of bacon

185g crème fraîche

Handful of fresh herbs, such as parsley or chives, chopped

Preheat the oven to 200°C (400°F), Gas Mark 6. Cut the potatoes into equal(ish) wedges and place them in a large baking tray in a single layer. Drizzle with some oil and season well with salt, pepper and as much paprika as you like. Pop in the oven and roast for about 35–40 minutes, taking them out halfway through to give them a good shake.

Meanwhile, put the mustard and maple syrup in a bowl and set aside.

Fry the bacon in a dry frying pan until the rashers are almost cooked and crisp, then take the pan off the heat. Using a brush, brush the mustard mixture over one side of the bacon, then flip the bacon over so the mustard side is facing down and pop it back into the pan and cook for a minute or so until the bacon is just the crispiness you like it. Repeat with the other side of the bacon and set aside.

Put the crème fraîche into a bowl and set aside. Take the potato wedges out of the oven and rip the bacon up over them. Add the herbs to the crème fraîche and serve with the potato wedges.

Oven-roast broccoli with chilli & mint

Roasting completely changes the flavour of certain vegetables, and broccoli is transformed when cooked this way. Serves 4 *(V)*

2 broccoli heads

Extra-virgin olive oil, for drizzling

3–4 small red chillies, deseeded and finely sliced

Salt and freshly ground black pepper

½ bunch of fresh mint

Preheat the oven to 200°C (400°F), Gas Mark 6. Break the broccoli into large bite-sized pieces and cut the stalks into 5mm circles. Scatter the broccoli over a baking tray, drizzle with some olive oil, throw over the chillies and season with salt and pepper. Bake in the oven for about 10 minutes, or until the pieces are turning golden brown.

Take the broccoli out of the oven, sprinkle over some mint leaves and serve hot. Great with any meat or fish dish or as part of a big veggie fiesta plate.

Hasselback tatties

These are just like a regular baked potato with a little bit extra and really good if you want to impress. The trick to getting the right effect is in not cutting all the way down. I first had these tatties years ago in a restaurant in Sweden. Serves 4 *(V)*

4 medium potatoes, unpeeled

Oil, for drizzling

Salt and freshly ground black pepper

Few sprigs of fresh thyme or rosemary (optional)

4 knobs of butter

Preheat the oven to 220°C (425°F), Gas Mark 7. Place a potato on a chopping board. If it does not stay still and keeps rolling around, slice off a little from the bottom so it will sit stable. Now with the longest side facing you, start at one end of the potato and make small cuts in the potato (as shown in the photo) at about 5mm intervals, all the way along the potato without going all the way through. Repeat with the remaining potatoes, then place them on a baking tray and fan them out a little so the slices do not stick together too much. Now drizzle with oil, trying to get some into the slits and season with a good amount of salt and pepper. For extra flavour, slot some thyme or rosemary into the slits.

Cook the potatoes in the oven for 50–60 minutes or until a knife prodded into the underside of one glides in easily and the potatoes are fully cooked.

Take the potatoes out of the oven and serve immediately with a knob of butter on top.

Root vegetable rosemary rösti with a chive & cracked black pepper crème fraîche

Crunchy patties of grated vegetables, a nice easy one to do for a supper accompaniment. Makes 8 rösti *(V)*

- 2 medium parsnips, about 350g, peeled and grated
- 1 medium sweet potato, about 300g, peeled and grated
- 1 medium carrot, about 175g, peeled and grated
- 100g plain flour
- 1 tbsp finely chopped fresh rosemary
- Sea salt and freshly ground black pepper
- 2 eggs, lightly beaten
- 2 tbsp sunflower oil
- 25g butter

Chive & cracked black pepper crème fraîche

- 125g crème fraîche
- 3 tbsp finely chopped fresh chives
- Juice of ½ lime

Place the grated parsnips, sweet potato and carrot in a large bowl and toss the flour, rosemary and plenty of salt and pepper through. Add the beaten eggs and mix well. Divide the mixture into 8 even-sized pieces and shape each one into a patty about 10cm in diameter and 1cm thick. To do this, I squeeze each portion into a ball and flatten it into this shape and size between the palms of my hands while trying to keep the edges as neat as possible. You can also use a palette knife to help make the sides more even and compact. Place each rösti onto a round of greaseproof paper, as this will make it easier to put them into the frying pan. At this stage you can refrigerate the röstis until ready to cook, if preparing in advance.

When ready to cook the röstis, preheat the oven to 180°C (350°F), Gas Mark 4. Heat half the oil and butter in a large non-stick frying pan over a medium heat and gently cook half of the röstis for 3–4 minutes on each side, turning them over carefully, until golden brown and beginning to set. Transfer them to a baking sheet and repeat with the remaining oil, butter and röstis. Bake the röstis in the oven for 15–20 minutes, or until completely cooked through.

Meanwhile, prepare the crème fraîche by simply putting the crème fraîche in a bowl and stirring through the chives, lime juice and enough seasoning to taste.

Serve the röstis on a large platter with a bowl of the chive and pepper crème fraîche for people to help themselves.

Baked mushroom, chestnut & pea 'risotto' with truffle oil

Truffles are amazing mushrooms from Italy, but they are very expensive. However, you can buy oil infused with truffles. This oil is one of life's great pleasures. I was introduced to it a few years ago and since then I have not looked back. The oil is not cheap, you get a teensy weensy bottle for about £4, but because the flavour is so intense you only need to use a small drizzle. Not being the most patient of chefs, I love this cheat's risotto: a little bit of stirring first, then straight into the oven to finish off. Serves 4–6

- 10–12g dried wild porcini mushrooms
- 200ml warm water
- Large knob of butter
- 150g chestnut mushrooms, wiped and finely sliced (or wild if they have them)
- 150g tinned whole chestnuts, broken up a little
- Salt and freshly ground black pepper
- 400g Arborio rice
- Good glug of dry white wine
- 700ml good-quality vegetable or chicken stock
- 1 bay leaf
- 100g Parmesan cheese (or use vegetarian Parmesan-style cheese)
- Handful of frozen peas
- Small handful of fresh thyme leaves
- Drizzle of truffle oil (optional)

Equipment

Large casserole or ovenproof dish, about 19 x 26cm and 5cm deep

Put the dried wild mushrooms in a mug, pour over the warm water and leave to soak for a good 20 minutes.

Preheat the oven to 200°C (400°F), Gas Mark 6. Melt the butter in a medium pan over a medium heat until it starts to sizzle, then add the fresh mushrooms and cook for 3–5 minutes. Add the chestnuts and some pepper (the Parmesan, which is added a little later is very salty, so there is no need to add any salt). Add the rice and stir everything together well, then add the wine. Turn up the heat and boil until most of the wine has evaporated. Now add the stock and bay leaf and return to the boil.

Meanwhile, place a sieve over a small bowl and tip the dried mushrooms and the soaking liquid into it. Pour the liquid in with the rice, then roughly chop the porcini mushrooms and add them to the rice.

Now tip the mixture into the casserole or ovenproof dish and cook, uncovered, in the oven for 20 minutes. After 20 minutes take the dish out of the oven, add the Parmesan cheese, peas and thyme and mix together well. Return to the oven and cook for a further 15–20 minutes, checking after 15 minutes to see if any more liquid is needed. If it is dry, just add a little water.

Once it is cooked, take the dish out of the oven and season to taste. I love to drizzle mine with truffle oil.

This dish is fabulously filling and a firm favourite in my house.

Extra thin & crispy goat's cheese tart with spinach & thyme pesto

This is really a posh pizza minus the time spent on making a real bread base. Making a crunchy crispy filo base in this way has been a very useful item in my foodie repertoire and toppings such as bananas with toffee sauce, four cheeses with some chopped fresh herbs or caramelised onions with mozzarella and basil have all seen their way through my kitchen. For something even more different before baking, cut the filo into circles or heart shapes for individual portions. Serves 6

½ x 270g packet of filo pastry (preferably not frozen; you can freeze the leftover pastry for use later)

1½ handfuls of fresh thyme leaves, plus extra for sprinkling (optional)

50g melted butter or light olive oil spray

1 large tomato, finely sliced

200g goat's cheese log, cut into 2.5mm-thick slices

Spinach pesto

Handful of spinach leaves

Handful of pine nuts, toasted (I found some pre-toasted at the supermarket, or pan-fry them for 3 minutes, until toasted)

1 clove of garlic, peeled

20–30ml extra-virgin olive oil

60g Parmesan cheese (or use vegetarian Parmesan-style cheese)

Salt and freshly ground black pepper

Preheat the oven to 200°C (400°F), Gas Mark 6. Lay one filo sheet on top of a flat (preferably non-stick) baking tray, sprinkle with a little thyme, if using, and place another filo sheet on top. Dab a little melted butter roughly over the tart, especially at the edges since they are prone to burning, and sprinkle with more thyme, if using. Repeat until you have four layers of pastry. Place another flat baking tray on top of the pastry and cook in the oven for 10–15 minutes, keeping a close eye on it.

Meanwhile, make the pesto by blending the spinach, pine nuts, garlic, olive oil and Parmesan together in a food processor. Season to taste.

Take the pastry base out of the oven. If the edges look like they are getting too dark, brush them with a little more melted butter, then spread the pesto over the pastry, leaving a 2cm border. Place the tomato and the goat's cheese slices in alternate layers, sprinkle with a little more thyme, if using, and bake in the oven for about 15 minutes, or until the goat's cheese begins to melt.

Take the tart out of the oven. I find that the bottom of the tart can get a little oily, so to combat this, I cut a slice of the tart and before serving put it on some kitchen paper to soak up any oil. Serve straightaway with a large green salad and a chilled Italian white wine.

Lemony basil spaghetti with mascarpone, chilli & chives

Now where would I be without old faithful spaghetti to save the day at dinner time, when there are hungry mouths waiting to be fed? This recipe is a fail-safe mealtime shortcut and makes a frequent appearance on our table. Serves 4–5

450g dried spaghetti or homemade pasta (see page 67)

220g frozen petit pois

3 red chillies, deseeded and finely diced

200g mascarpone

1 bunch of fresh basil, leaves only

1 bunch of fresh mint, leaves only

2 very large handfuls of pine nuts, toasted (I found some pre-toasted at the supermarket, or pan-fry them for 3 minutes, until toasted)

1 bunch of fresh chives, finely chopped

Juice of 1 lemon

Salt and freshly ground black pepper

Extra-virgin olive oil, for drizzling (optional)

Parmesan shavings, to serve (optional)

Cook the spaghetti in a large pan of water according to the manufacturer's instructions or if you are cooking homemade pasta, follow the recipe on page 64. Five minutes before the spaghetti is ready, throw in the petit pois and cook for 3–5 minutes. Drain the peas and pasta and return everything to the pan. Add the chillies and gently stir in the mascarpone.

Rip up the basil and mint leaves and add them to the pasta, then sprinkle the pine nuts on top together with the chopped chives. Stir very gently and not using too many 'stirs' so the mixture does not go all mooshy.

To serve, using a pair of tongs, lift up some of the pasta and place it in the middle of a warmed serving plate piled high. For me, this looks so much nicer than just putting it flat on a plate. Add a good squeeze of lemon juice and salt and pepper to taste. If you like, drizzle some olive oil over the top.

Some Parmesan shavings finish this dish off very nicely. I use a vegetable peeler to shave off large pieces and balance them on top of the pasta.

Roasted beetroot salad with orange, goat's cheese, mint & toasted hazelnuts

With all this hearty cooking, it is sometimes nice to have a something light in the evening instead. I am mad about salads and have fun experimenting with the different flavours and textures to make something just a little bit different. When toasting the hazelnuts, keep a close eye on them, as they can burn easily. Serves 4 as a main or 8 as a starter *(V)*

4 large beetroot, unpeeled

About 125g mixed leaves (rocket and baby spinach, or the beet leaves if tender enough)

Handful of fresh mint leaves

2 oranges, segmented (peel the oranges and rip off segments)

400g goat's cheese log, sliced into 4 thick rounds

50g hazelnuts, roughly chopped and toasted (fry them in a dry pan for 2 minutes, or until toasted)

Dressing

(makes about 125ml)

4 tbsp balsamic vinegar

3 tbsp maple syrup or runny honey

Good pinch of mustard powder or a small dollop of English mustard

2 tbsp extra virgin olive oil

Sea salt and freshly ground black pepper

Preheat the oven to 220°C (425°F), Gas Mark 7. Wrap each beetroot individually in a square of foil and place them on a baking tray. Pop them in the oven for 1–1¼ hours, or until the beetroot is nice and soft. Take out of the oven, carefully remove the foil and leave the beetroot until cool enough to handle. Top and tail them, peel off the skin and cut each one into eight wedges.

To make the dressing, mix the vinegar, maple syrup or honey, mustard and olive oil together with salt and pepper to taste. I find the easiest way to do this is by putting everything into a screw-top jar, putting the lid on and shaking the jar like mad.

Put the salad leaves and mint in a large bowl and coat lightly with some of the dressing. Divide the dressed leaves between four large (or eight smaller) serving bowls and arrange the orange segments and beetroot pieces in the salad. I tuck some on top and put some underneath so they are evenly dispersed. Place the goat's cheese slices on top and sprinkle with the toasted hazelnuts. Drizzle with the rest of the dressing, sprinkle a little salt and pepper over and serve.

Asparagus, tarragon & mint omelette

This dish is such a beauty. When I was testing the recipes for the book, it was the height of summer and I made use of the abundance of summer herbs and vegetables, but to make this more seasonal during the winter months, I often make it with broccoli instead of asparagus and parsley and thyme instead of the mint and tarragon – I find it equally delicious. Serves 4

2 medium potatoes, finely grated and washed

Oil, for cooking

7–8 medium eggs

Freshly ground black pepper

2 very generous pinches of cayenne pepper

60g Parmesan cheese, grated (or use vegetarian Parmesan-style cheese)

Small handful of fresh mint leaves, roughly chopped

Few fresh tarragon leaves, roughly chopped

Large knob of butter

About 8 asparagus spears, trimmed a little at the end

Handful of frozen petit pois or peas

Equipment

25cm ovenproof frying pan or sandwich tin (one with a fixed base)

Preheat the oven to 150°C (300°F), Gas Mark 2. Put the grated potatoes between two pieces of kitchen paper and squeeze to get rid of all the excess liquid.

Put a little oil in a frying pan, add the potatoes and cook over a high heat for about 5–8 minutes, or until they begin to soften. It is fine if they get a bit toasty and golden brown.

When the potatoes are almost ready, whisk the eggs in a bowl. If you can get a good amount of air into the eggs, they will rise a little like a soufflé when baked in the oven. Add the pepper, cayenne, Parmesan, mint and tarragon and whisk a little more. Melt the knob of butter in a frying pan then pour in the egg mixture and cook over a low–medium heat for 3–4 minutes. Add the asparagus and peas to the egg mixture and place in the oven. If you do not have an ovenproof frying pan, transfer the mixture to the sandwich tin placed on a baking tray.

Cook in the oven for about 8–10 minutes, or until just cooked.
The cooking time will vary depending on how much you have whisked up the egg, so check after 8 minutes and see if it needs more time.

Serve immediately with a salad.

Spinach, rocket & Parmesan roulade with sun-dried tomato & pine nut filling

Being a fan of Swiss rolls, I wanted to come up with something that was rolled but savoury. A bit of tinkering around with my Swiss roll tin, and I came up with this gem. The roulade can be made in the morning and then just taken out of the fridge when ready to serve. Serves 4–6

- Knob of butter
- 300g baby leaf spinach
- 5 eggs, separated
- 100g Parmesan cheese (or use vegetarian Parmesan-style cheese), finely grated, plus 1 tbsp for sprinkling
- Pinch of freshly grated nutmeg
- Sea salt and freshly ground black pepper
- 250g crème fraîche
- 100g sun-dried tomatoes in oil, drained and finely chopped
- Small handful of pine nuts, toasted (I found some pre-toasted at the supermarket, or pan-fry them for 3 minutes, until toasted)
- 60g bag of wild rocket

Equipment

23 x 32cm Swiss roll tin

Preheat the oven to 180°C (350°F), Gas Mark 4. Line the Swiss roll tin with baking parchment, leaving some extra length hanging over the edges so it is easy to lift out once cooked.

Melt the butter in a large pan over a medium heat. When it begins to sizzle, add the spinach and cook for about 1 minute, tossing until wilted. Tip the spinach into a colander and, with the back of a spoon, squeeze out the excess moisture well until it is as dry as possible. Next, blitz the spinach in a food processor or mini blender until very finely chopped.

Transfer the chopped spinach to a large bowl and add the egg yolks, Parmesan and nutmeg. Season with salt and pepper and stir together until well mixed.

Whisk the egg whites in another bowl until stiff. They do not need to be as stiff as a meringue mix, but about three-quarters of the way there. Stir a spoonful of the whites into the spinach mixture to loosen it a little and then, using a plastic spatula or metal spoon, gently fold the remaining whites through until well combined.

Pour the mixture into the prepared tin from a low height so as not to knock all of the air out of it. Smooth it out gently with the back of a spoon so it is level, then cook in the oven for 10–15 minutes, or until the egg mix is just set all over. Remove and leave to stand in the tin for 5–10 minutes before running a knife down the sides to loosen it.

▶

Spinach, rocket & Parmesan roulade with sun-dried tomato & pine nut filling

(continued)

Put a piece of baking parchment a little bigger than the roulade on the work surface and sprinkle it evenly with the extra grated Parmesan. Remove the cooked roulade from the tin using the baking parchment and turn it top side down on the new baking parchment. Carefully peel off the baking parchment and leave the roulade to cool completely.

Meanwhile, mix the crème fraîche, sun-dried tomatoes and pine nuts together in a bowl and season to taste. When the roulade is cool, gently spread the filling over, leaving a border of about 1cm all the way round, then sprinkle the rocket over evenly.

With one of the longest sides facing you, begin to roll up the roulade away from you, using the baking parchment to help lift it as you go. Try to do it as tightly as you can for an impressive-looking finish. Once you have rolled it up, carefully transfer the roulade onto a plate, seam side down.

This is a great starter dish – bring it to the table whole and slice it up in front of guests. You can get 10–12 fairly thick slices from it. This roulade can be made ahead and stored in the fridge.

Stilton, pear & poppy seed tartlets

I am a pear lover and they crop up many times in this book. This classic combo of pear and Stilton is, in my eyes, a glorious feast for the senses, with poppy seeds thrown in for extra crunch. Serves 6 *(V)*

500g packet of puff pastry

Plain flour, for dusting

3 perfectly ripe pears

Juice of ½ lime or small lemon

1 egg, lightly beaten

200g Stilton or dolcelatte cheese

Freshly ground black pepper

1 squidge of honey or maple syrup (optional)

½ tsp poppy seeds

1 tbsp snipped fresh chives

Extra-virgin olive oil, to serve

Preheat the oven to 220°C (425°F), Gas Mark 7. Roll out the pastry on a floured work surface into a 25.5 x 30.5cm rectangle the thickness of a £1 coin. Trim the edges with a sharp knife to neaten, then with the longer length of the pastry running away from you, cut it in half. Divide each strip evenly into three pieces, cutting in the opposite direction. Arrange the six rectangular pieces on a large non-stick baking tray and pop them in the fridge for 20 minutes or in the freezer for 10 minutes.

Meanwhile, prepare the pears. Peel them, cut them in half down the length and remove the core with a Parisienne scoop or apple corer. Squeeze a little lime or lemon juice over them to stop them going brown. Slice each pear half across into about 1cm-thick slices, being careful to keep each in their pear shape. I love the way this looks on the tart.

Remove the pastry from the fridge or freezer and brush the tops with the beaten egg, making sure it does not run down the sides. If it does run a little, just wipe it off – this will stop the egg from sticking the layers of pastry together as it cooks and prevent the pastry rising nicely.

Crumble a third of the cheese over the pastry pieces, then carefully arrange a pear half in the centre of each. Squish them down to fan them out slightly, then scatter over the rest of the cheese and season with pepper. The cheese can be salty, so I tend not to add extra. Brush a squidge of honey or maple syrup over, if you like (I can't help myself!).

Now cook the tartlets in the oven for about 15–20 minutes, or until the pastry is well puffed up and is nice and firm and golden brown on the sides and the cheese is catching colour.

Take out of the oven and leave to cool a little before transferring to serving plates. Scatter the poppy seeds and chives over and serve drizzled with a little olive oil and a dressed green salad.

Desserts

Which is your favourite type of food? For me, wrestling for pole position with bread, it has to be pud. I love the cheekily named spotted dick for its doughy pillowy spiciness and to be frank, I could eat all the steamed chocolate pudding with warm Mars bar sauce by myself in one sitting (well, almost!). My biscuits of choice are chocolate digestives and so making a cheesecake out of them was a must, but the scene-stealer, which is so very easy to make, is my big fat tipsy trifle, dripping with delicious ingredients such as fresh strawberries, white chocolate, madeira sponge (shop-bought) and crunched up amaretti biscuits. The desserts in this chapter are some of my current faves, which make frequent appearances on the table Chez LP. I hope you will like them too.

'The belly rules the mind'

Spanish proverb

Caramelised banana bread & butter pudding with toasted pecans

I wasn't really a fan of bread and butter pudding until I added some extra bits and pieces to it – the banana caramelises as it bakes and the pecans add some extra crunch. It is a tasty, easy, comfort food dish. Serves 6–8 *(V)*

75g butter, at room temperature

1 medium loaf of crusty white bread, cut into 8–10 slices about 2cm thick

400ml double cream

300ml crème fraîche

75g soft light brown sugar, plus 25g extra for sprinkling

Grated zest of 1 lemon

Seeds from 1 vanilla pod or a couple of drops of vanilla extract

1 tsp ground cinnamon

4 eggs

2 bananas, peeled and cut into 1cm thick slices

100g pecan nuts

Equipment

4-litre capacity baking dish, about 25 x 30cm and 7.5cm deep

Preheat the oven to 180°C (350°F), Gas Mark 4. Grease the ovenproof dish with a little of the butter.

Use the remaining butter to butter the bread slices on one side. Cut the slices in half diagonally and arrange them in the prepared baking dish. You can arrange the slices of bread any way you like; I usually put them cut side down (so the point is standing up) and side by side, overlapping slightly in rows, so they are quite tightly packed. Fill the whole dish, but you may need more or less depending on your dish size.

Next, put the cream, crème fraîche, the 75g sugar, lemon zest, vanilla, cinnamon and eggs in a large jug and beat with a wooden spoon until smooth and well mixed.

Now put the banana slices and pecans between the slices of bread, with a few landing on top. Pour the liquid over the bread and allow it to soak through for a few seconds, then use the back of a spoon to squidge everything down into the liquid. Finally, scatter the remaining sugar evenly over the top. Bake in the oven for 30–40 minutes, or until the mixture has just set and looks nicely caramelised.

Serve at once. This is delicious with a little more fresh cream poured over but also really good with some melted plain chocolate.

Shameless, flourless, moist & sticky chocolate cake

A gluten-free wonder with a brilliant taste. Serve this delicious cake for a dinner party or a special family gathering, drizzled with double cream or with scoops of vanilla ice cream. Serves 8–10 *(V)*

165g butter

180g dark chocolate (at least 70% cocoa solids), grated

6 eggs, separated

130g caster sugar

130g ground almonds

Chocolate frosting

150g dark chocolate (at least 70% cocoa solids), broken into pieces

300g butter, softened

225g icing sugar

Equipment

25cm springform cake tin

Preheat the oven to 170°C (325°F), Gas Mark 3. Line the cake tin with greaseproof paper.

Melt the butter in a medium pan over a gentle heat. Take off the heat, add the grated chocolate and leave to melt.

In a large bowl, whisk the egg yolks until they are doubled in size, then slowly add half of the caster sugar, whisking hard all the time. Once the mix is light and foamy, add the chocolate and fold in with a plastic spatula or metal spoon to combine.

Put the egg whites in a large bowl and whisk until they begin to turn opaque, then, while continuing to whisk gradually, add the remaining sugar. Fold the egg whites into the chocolate mix with a spatula or metal spoon, then carefully stir in the ground almonds.

Dollop the mixture into the prepared tin and bake on the middle shelf of the oven for 30–40 minutes, or until the cake is cooked but still a little gooey in the centre.

Meanwhile, to make the frosting, melt the chocolate in a heatproof bowl set over a pan of hot water, making sure the base of the bowl does not touch the water; or put the chocolate in a plastic bowl and melt in the microwave at 30-second intervals, stirring in between each one. Once the chocolate has melted, set it aside to cool a little.

Beat the butter and icing sugar together in a bowl until light and fluffy, then add the cooled but still molten chocolate and stir well. Set aside.

Take the cake out of the oven and leave to cool completely in the tin. Once cold, turn the cake out on a serving plate. Don't worry if the cake collapses a little in the middle. Now slather the chocolate frosting over the top and sides and serve immediately.

Sauternes, cardamom & ginger poached pears

A cracking dish packed with flavour, these pears are super easy to make ahead of time and all you need to do is take them out of the fridge when you are ready to serve. If you can't find a bottle of Sauternes, any dessert wine will do. Serves 4–6 *(V)*

- 4–6 almost-ripe pears, such as Comice or Conference
- 1 x 375ml bottle of Sauternes
- 100g soft light brown sugar
- Grated zest of 1 lemon
- 1 x 2cm piece of fresh ginger, peeled and grated
- 4 cardamom pods, crushed (fry them in a dry pan for 3–4 minutes, to bring out the flavour, if you like)
- 1 cinnamon stick
- Seeds of 1 vanilla pod or a few drops of vanilla extract
- Twist of black pepper
- 2 cloves
- About 200ml water

Honey mascarpone

- 150g mascarpone
- Few squidges of honey
- Toasted hazelnuts, for sprinkling, optional (fry them in a dry pan for 2 minutes, or until toasted)

Peel the pears, leaving the stems intact and cut a little bit off the base of them if they do not stand up. You can remove the core from the bottom with a sharp knife if you like, but I tend not to bother.

Put the wine, sugar, lemon zest, ginger, cardamom, cinnamon, vanilla, pepper and cloves into a medium pan, then arrange the pears in a single layer and put the pan over a high heat. Pour in enough water to cover the pears, then bring to the boil. Boil like mad for 3–4 minutes to get rid of the very strong alcoholic taste, then immediately turn the heat down so the liquid is just simmering. Leave to simmer for about 20 minutes, then turn off the heat and set the pears aside in the liquid to cool.

Once the pears are cool, they can be stored in the poaching liquid in the fridge for 2–3 days, so they are a great make-ahead-of-time dish.

To finish, put the mascarpone in a bowl and gently stir in the honey. Sprinkle over some toasted hazelnuts, if using, and serve with the pears.

A very spotted dick

Rude name, delicious pud – enough said. Serves 6

Filling

165g raisins

50g pecans, toasted and roughly chopped

1 tsp ground mixed spice

Grated zest of ½–1 lemon

50g butter

1 tbsp brandy (optional)

Dough

160g self-raising flour, plus extra for dusting

60g suet (or use vegetarian suet if you are vegetarian)

Pinch of salt

2 tbsp soft light brown sugar

40g raisins

75–100ml cream or enough to make a moist dough

Oil, for oiling

Preheat the oven to 180°C (350°F), Gas Mark 4. Pull all the ingredients for the filling in a bowl, mix together and set aside.

For the dough, put the flour, suet, salt, sugar and raisins in a bowl and mix together, adding the cream bit by bit to make a soft, fairly moist dough. Roll the dough out on a floured surface to a rectangle about the same size as a piece of A4 paper.

If you have a steamer pan, pop it on the hob a third full of water and bring to the boil. If you do not have a steamer, place a pan filled with water on the hob with a colander sitting inside it. Make sure that the colander does not touch the top of the water, then pop a lid or a baking tray on top.

Spread the filling mixture all the way up to the edges of the dough, then with the shortest edges facing you, roll the pastry up, like a Swiss roll. Once rolled, place the spotted dick in a large piece of double oiled foil. Make a 2cm pleat across the foil to allow for the pudding to rise, and roll it up like a cracker so that it is airtight. Secure the foil with string. Now place the spotted dick into the steamer over a gentle heat and cook for 1¾–2 hours.

If the spotted dick will not fit inside the steamer or pan, cut it in half and roll each half up in foil, then put them side by side in the steamer or pan. Cover with a lid and check the level of the water every 30 minutes or so, to make sure it has not bubbled away.

Once the cooking time is up, take the pudding out of the steamer, leave it to cool for a moment, then unwrap it to check to see if it is cooked.

Once cooked, cut into large slices and serve with some old-fashioned shop-bought custard.

My big fat tipsy trifle

I have a massive trifle dish I bought from a department store, which is perfect for this recipe. If you are using a standard glass dish, reduce the amounts by a third. This trifle is a real showstopper and so very simple to make – ready from start to finish in about 30–40 minutes. Serves about 10 (V)

2 x shop-bought Madeira loaf cakes

150ml Amaretti, Cognac, Grand Marnier, Cointreau or any strong liqueur (optional)

800g strawberries, hulled and cut in half lengthways

250g amaretti biscuits, crumbled

Seeds of 1 vanilla pod or a few drops of vanilla extract

100g icing sugar

900ml double cream

200g white chocolate, grated

Equipment

Large trifle dish or glass bowl

Put the trifle dish on a large tray to make it easier to carry. Slice one of the Madeira cakes into 5mm slices and use a few of the slices to line the bottom of the dish. Make sure they are nice and tight and in a single layer, so squidge down any bits that are standing up too high. Brush the sponge with some of the alcohol of your choice, if using, then take a few strawberries that are roughly the same size, if possible, and turn one half upside down and put it on the outer edge of the cake so it is pressing up to the glass. Repeat all the way round the dish. Sprinkle some crumbled amaretti biscuits on top of the cake mixture to a third of the way up the strawberries.

Put the vanilla, icing sugar and cream in a bowl and whip until thick, almost like cream cheese but a little looser. Spread a third of the cream on top of the strawberries and crumbled biscuits and smooth it down flat with a spoon. The cream should come up to only a couple of millimetres or above the level of the top of the strawberries. The amaretti biscuits do stick to the spoon while spreading the cream on, so I use a small knife to just scrape them off. Stand back from your evolving masterpiece and have a look to see if the cream is level. If it is not, use a piece of kitchen paper to wipe around the edge of the bowl, then sprinkle with a layer of grated chocolate.

Now repeat each layer until the bowl is full, finishing with a layer of strawberries. Set aside.

►

My big fat tipsy trifle
(continued)

For a bit of fun, try flambéing the trifle before serving it. Flambéing is very easy and the flames die out as soon as the alcohol has burnt out, but I always feel more comfortable with a large pan lid nearby just in case I need to put out the flame. The flame is similar to when a Christmas pudding is lit up or when a sambuca shot is lit by the barman. If using alcohol, you can carefully pour the alcohol over the trifle at the table and light it with a match. Sometimes it works, sometimes it doesn't, but it's fun to try. Let the flames die out before serving the trifle. The top layer of cream will have melted a little but it will still taste delicious!

Frozen raspberry ripple parfait 'ice cream'

No ice-cream maker required! This dessert is simply heavenly – so, so soft, rich and tasty. You can serve it on its own or with hot melted chocolate. Not technically a proper ice cream but it is delicious all the same. A bit of bowl juggling is required in the making of this recipe and it also should be made the day before you need it. Once it is made and frozen, I always remove it from the freezer 10 minutes or so before serving, so it is easier to cut into slices. Serves 4 *(V)*

250g frozen raspberries, thawed

110g caster sugar

2 very fresh egg whites or 125g pasteurised egg whites (available from the supermarket and best if serving this to kiddies, the infirm or the elderly)

200ml double cream or whipping cream

Seeds of 1 vanilla pod and a couple of drops of vanilla extract

Fresh raspberries, to serve

Equipment

16 x 8cm loaf tin

Line the loaf tin with clingfilm so it hangs over the sides and set aside. If the clingfilm keeps lifting up when lining the loaf tin, I find it sticks a bit better to the tin if I wet the tin first with a spray of water.

Blitz the berries in a blender, then put a sieve over a bowl and pour the berry mixture into it. Squish the berry mix through the sieve with a wooden spoon, then set it aside. Discard the pips in the sieve.

Put the sugar into another bowl and add half of the egg whites. Whisk like mad until the mixture is stiff. Add the rest of the egg whites and keep on whisking until the mixture is very stiff, brilliant white and super shiny. Set aside.

In another bowl, whip the double cream until it is thick, then add the vanilla. Spoon the cream into the egg white mixture and fold together. Pour in the raspberry mixture and fold together roughly to give ripples.

Now tip the mixture into the prepared loaf tin, smooth over the top and place in the freezer until firm.

To remove from the tin, take out of the freezer 10 minutes before serving, lift out of the tin using the clingfilm, invert onto a dish or board and serve in slices with some fresh raspberries.

White chocolate mousse with crème fraîche & stem ginger

When I first made these mousses, I ended up eating nearly half of the mixture before it made its way into the glasses to set. You can make these up to 24 hours in advance and whip them out just as you are ready to serve. Makes 4 large glasses *(V)*

150g crème fraîche

300ml double cream

400g white chocolate, melted (see page 195)

3 x 1cm pieces of stem ginger, finely chopped

Put the crème fraîche in one bowl and the cream in another. Mix the crème fraiche until it loosens up and becomes a bit thinner. Whip the double cream until it is almost the same consistency as the crème fraîche. Making sure these two mixtures are more or less the same consistency will give it the best chance of not becoming lumpy. Now tip the crème fraîche into the whipped cream mixture and stir them together to combine.

Put a dollop of the crème fraîche mixture into the melted chocolate and stir it together. Add another dollop of the crème fraîche mixture to the chocolate and stir. Repeat, stirring well until all the crème fraîche and chocolate has been combined and the mixture looks silky and smooth, then fold in the stem ginger. Pour into four glasses and pop in the fridge to set for a minimum of 1 hour. For a very gingery taste, spoon a little extra ginger syrup over the top of the mousse just before serving.

Extra gooey pecan pie with brown sugar pastry

A super simple dessert, but if you are pressed for time, use shop bought sweet pastry and it will still taste absolutely scrummy. Serves 6–8 *(V)*

175g fridge-cold butter, cut into cubes

Good pinch of salt

375g plain flour, plus extra for dusting

1 tbsp soft dark brown sugar

1 egg, lightly beaten

Seeds of ½ vanilla pod or a couple of drops of vanilla extract

1 tbsp ice-cold water (optional)

or 1 x 375g packet of ready-made sweet pastry

Filling

60g butter

150g golden syrup

200g soft dark brown sugar

4 medium eggs

200–300g pecan nuts

Equipment

25cm diameter pie dish or loose-based flan tin, about 3cm deep

If you are making the pastry, put the butter, salt and flour in a food processor and process until it resembles fine breadcrumbs. Add the sugar and whiz briefly. Add the beaten egg and vanilla and process again until the pastry starts to come together, adding a little ice-cold water if necessary. Once the pastry starts to come together, tip it into a bowl and bring it together with your hands. Alternatively, to make the pastry by hand, put the flour and butter in a bowl and, using your fingertips, rub the butter into the flour until it resembles breadcrumbs. Stir in the sugar and salt and mix together until it starts to clump together. I like to get my hands in and squeeze it all together to see how it feels and if it feels too dry I add the egg and water. Add the vanilla and mix until the mixture starts to leave the sides of the bowl and comes together. Form the pastry into a flattened circle and rest in the fridge for 30 minutes–1 hour or until firm.

Preheat the oven to 180°C (350°F), Gas Mark 4. Roll the pastry out on a well-floured board to just under £1 thickness. If the pastry has become too hard, you can chop it up into 3–4 pieces and knead it together to soften. If it is too soft or almost wet, add a little flour and knead it for a minute or so.

Place the rolling pin in the centre of the dough and fold the top half of the pastry over it, lift up the rolling pin and drape it over the pie dish or flan tin. Use a small ball of the pastry to ease the pastry into the corners of the tin, then use a sharp knife to trim off any excess pastry. If the pastry is very soft, put the tart case in the fridge for 20 minutes or in the freezer for 10 minutes.

►

Extra gooey pecan pie with brown sugar pastry (continued)

Scrunch up a piece of baking parchment slightly larger than the pastry, then unscrunch it and lay it down on the pastry. Fill with ceramic baking beans or dried beans and bake in the oven for 30 minutes, or until the pastry feels sandy. Sometimes after the 30 minutes is up I remove the beans and baking parchment and place it back in the oven for another 5 minutes, then take it out of the oven.

To make the filling, melt the butter in a medium pan, then take the pan off the heat and leave to cool slightly before adding the golden syrup, sugar and eggs. Mix together until well combined, then add the pecans and pour the filling into the tart case. To make the tart look very pretty, fold in half the pecans, then arrange the other half on top of the filling in an attractive pattern. I don't always have the time to do this, but rustic works well too!

Put the tart on a baking tray and bake in the oven for about 30 minutes, or until the centre of the tart no longer wobbles. Have a look at it after 20 minutes to see how it is doing and turn it around in the oven to make sure the tart cooks evenly. Once it is cooked, take it out of the oven and leave to cool.

Serve with vanilla ice cream. This pie is also delicious eaten cold the next day.

Chocolate digestive cheesecake with white icing

My mum would go shopping once a week on Monday morning, and during the holidays it was an event that I did not want to miss, as my brother and I were allowed one packet of biscuits each, that were to last the whole week. My brother would choose Rich Tea and I would choose chocolate digestives – milk, not plain. On cold evenings, I would take a chocolate biscuit and sit by the electric heater in the living room, watching TV. I would hold the biscuit up to the heater (being careful not to burn myself, of course!) and wait until all of the chocolate had melted and then slowly lick off the rich warm chocolate. I have moved on a bit with my chocolate digestive biscuits these days and have used them as the base of this decadent cheesecake, which I find hard to resist. This cheesecake one is a stunner and wonderfully rich, so it will serve a good crowd for dessert. Serves 10 *(V)*

1 x 400g packet of chocolate digestives, crushed to fine crumbs

75g butter, melted and cooled slightly

4 x 200g tubs cream cheese

Icing sugar, to taste

400g milk chocolate (at least 35% cocoa solids), or you can use a mixture of 300g milk and 100g dark chocolate (at least 70% cocoa solids)

1 tsp vegetable oil

100g white chocolate

Equipment

23cm springform tin

Piping bag fitted with a very small nozzle (optional)

Mix the crushed biscuits and melted and cooled butter together, squeezing them together with the back of the wooden spoon until everything is well incorporated. Use something flat to make it even. I use the bottom of a cake tin, which is slightly smaller than the springform tin and then press down very hard all the way around so that the biscuits are flat and even.

Put the cream cheese and icing sugar in a bowl and mix together gently this will take only a few turns of the spoon. Melt the chocolate in a heatproof bowl set over a pan of simmering water, making sure the bottom of the bowl does not touch the water, or you can do this in the microwave. Pour a quarter of the chocolate into a jug, add the oil then set aside and keep warm. If you have a microwave the chocolate can be blasted for 20 seconds before it needs to be used again if not, just cover it with a clean tea towel and set it somewhere warm.

Now add a large dollop of the cream cheese mixture into the bowl of chocolate and stir well to combine. Add another dollop of cream cheese mixture to the chocolate mixture and stir to combine. Keep adding the

▶

Chocolate digestive cheesecake with white icing
(continued)

cream cheese mixture, one dollop at a time, and mixing it like mad until the chocolate mixture begins to look uniform, smooth and silky. At this point, tip all of the cream cheese mixture into the chocolate mixture and mix together until it is completely incorporated. Tip the mixture on top of the biscuit base and use the back of a large spoon to smooth the top. Press it down well so there are no gaps. Pop the cheesecake in the fridge for about 20 minutes or the freezer for 10 minutes, or until the chocolate top is beginning to firm up a little. It won't be totally hard, but it will begin to feel a bit tacky.

Five minutes before the cheesecake is ready, melt the white chocolate and make sure the jug of milk chocolate is nice and runny. Now remove the cheesecake from the fridge and, acting quickly, pour the milk chocolate over the top of it, spreading it out as you go until the top is completely covered. For a smooth finish, pick up the cheesecake and tilt it back and forth, letting the chocolate run over and cover the cream cheese filling. Now drizzle white chocolate lines across the top about 2cm apart. The neatest way to do this is by putting the chocolate into a piping bag fitted with a very small nozzle. Place the cheesecake so the lines are running towards you, then take a cocktail stick and drag it from left to right, making lines from left to right 2cm apart so you have a grid. Using the cocktail stick, drag it from right to left between the toothpick lines that you have just made. You will need to do this quite quickly so the chocolate lines are still runny. Leave the cheesecake in a cool place to set for about 2 hours.

If you want to serve the cheesecake straightaway, run a knife around the inside of the tin and remove the outside of the tin.

Serve in wedges with a drizzle of single cream.

Steamed chocolate pudding with warm Mars bar sauce

I made this pudding recently and half of it was eaten by the family before it made it to the table. The pudding is so very moist and the Mars bar sauce is just out of this world; it is a chocolatey take on a steamed golden syrup pudding. Serves 6 *(V)*

- 225g soft light brown sugar
- 225g butter, softened
- 5 eggs
- Seeds of 1 vanilla pod or a couple of drops of vanilla extract
- 150g plain flour
- 12g or 1 almost tbsp baking powder
- 50g cocoa powder
- 60g ground almonds
- Pinch of salt
- Vegetable oil, for oiling (or use an oil spray)

Mars bar sauce

- 5 x standard size Mars bars
- 75g melted butter

Equipment

- 1.5-litre capacity pudding basin

Make sure the pudding basin fits comfortably inside a large pan with plenty of room for a lid. Put the sugar and butter in a large bowl and beat well. Add two eggs, the vanilla, half of the flour and the baking powder and beat well until it is combined. Add the remaining eggs, the rest of the flour and all of the cocoa and beat very well until combined. Add the ground almonds and salt and stir well. Set aside.

Put all the ingredients for the Mars bar sauce into a small pan and melt over a low heat, stirring from time to time so it does not burn. Once it has melted, pour a quarter of it into the bottom of the pudding basin and set it aside. Dollop the chocolate pudding mixture on top of the sauce.

Brush or spray a large piece of foil with vegetable oil and place it over the top of the pudding basin, making sure there is room for the pudding to rise during cooking. Secure the foil just under the rim of the bowl, about 3cm from the top, with a piece of string. The pudding basin needs to be lifted in and out of the big pan, and I usually get another piece of string and make a handle with it, so I can manoeuvre it around easily. Now lower the pudding basin into the large pan and put the kettle on to boil. Pour the hot water into the pan so that it comes halfway up the pudding basin. Turn the heat on so it is simmering very gently and cook for 1½ hours, checking the water level from time to time and topping up with boiling water from the kettle if necessary.

Five minutes before the pudding is ready, reheat the remaining sauce and keep warm. Remove the basin from the pan using the handle and cool for a moment, then take off the string and foil. Place a large plate on top of the basin and then using oven gloves turn the pudding upside down. Carefully remove the basin, and there's your pud! Pour over the sauce and serve. This is delicious with ice cream or a drizzle of single cream.

Cakes & Cookies

I have said many times that one of the reasons I got into cooking was so that I could lick out the bowl after I made a cake. And to this day that still rings true. Bring out a cake to friends or family and it seems to make everyone smile, and I find sinking the knife through the spongy moistness and serving up a slice or an individual cake to excited faces incredibly rewarding. The same goes for cookies, muffins and bars; from my oat couture granola bars, which are great for a quick-grab anytime snack, to the retro and revamped caramelised pineapple and rum upside-down cake (in which raspberries replace the classic glacé cherry). Not forgetting my Swiss roll bowl cake, a shortcut no-cook beauty made with shop-bought Swiss roll and shop-bought ice cream for those days when you don't feel like turning on the oven. The pièce de résistance in this chapter has to be the graffiti cake – a moist vanilla sponge adorned with some bright red edible art, which is really great fun to make!

'A balanced diet is a cookie in each hand'

Anonymous

Party time chocolate fridge cake

I have had this chocolate fridge cake lots of times with nuts, raisins and all manner of things in it, but I still like it just the way it is, with plain and delicious digestive biscuits, Maltesers and melted chocolate. It is a great one for little kids and grown-ups alike. Makes 16 squares *(V)*

125g butter

400g good-quality milk or plain chocolate, grated or chopped

2 dollops of golden syrup

250g digestive biscuits, lightly crushed

135g packet of Maltesers

Equipment

20cm square brownie tin or sandwich tin

Line the tin with baking parchment. Put the butter in a large pan and melt over a low heat. Add the chocolate and golden syrup and allow to melt for a couple of minutes, stirring. Take the pan off the heat and stir in the digestive biscuits and Maltesers until evenly mixed.

Tip the mixture into the prepared tin and flatten the top down as smoothly as possible with the back of a spoon. Cover and place in the fridge for a couple of hours or until it hardens. When ready to serve, remove from the tin and cut up into 16 even-sized squares.

Raspberry muffins with brown sugar topping

Frozen raspberries are a good staple to have in the freezer. Good for mixing into cakes, stirring through ice cream or, in the case of these, to add to a muffin mix. Having said that, you can vary this recipe if you like and use strawberries, blueberries or even blackberries instead. Makes 12 muffins *(V)*

- 350g self-raising flour
- 1 tsp bicarbonate of soda
- Pinch of salt
- 250g soft light brown sugar, plus extra 25g sugar for the topping
- 1 tsp ground cinnamon (optional)
- 350ml buttermilk (or regular milk with 1 tsp lemon juice and left for 5 minutes)
- 2 eggs, lightly beaten
- 150g butter, melted and cooled
- 200g raspberries (fresh or frozen)

Equipment

12-hole muffin tin

Preheat the oven to 200°C (400°F), Gas Mark 6. Line the muffin tin with paper muffin cases, or for a 'deli' feel cut out 12 squares of baking parchment about 15cm each and push them down into each hole. Cut out 12 more squares of the same size and push them down into the hole, but slightly staggered to give a pretty jagged top edge.

Put the flour, bicarbonate of soda, salt, the 250g sugar and cinnamon, if using, in a large bowl and stir a little to combine. Add the buttermilk, eggs and melted and cooled butter and stir everything together well to give a smooth, thick batter.

Reserve about 24 raspberries for the tops of the muffins, then add the remainder to the mixture and gently fold them into the mixture. If using frozen berries, you might need to break them apart before adding them into the mixture.

Dollop the mixture evenly between the prepared paper cases in the tin, then pop two of the reserved raspberries on top of each muffin, without pushing them in. I think it's nice to have a few visible and not all incorporated into the mix.

Bake on the middle shelf of the oven for 20 minutes or until cooked to a deep golden colour. Take the muffins out of the oven and sprinkle with the reserved brown sugar, then pop them back in again for 10 minutes or until the sugar is slightly golden.

Remove from the oven and leave to cool in the tin. They are delicious served either warm or cold.

Caramelised pineapple, rum & vanilla upside-down cake

Are you old enough to remember when pineapple upside-down cake was quite the thing? Sitting all proud in the centre of the table amidst pretty white doilies and heavily patterned plates? Way back then, I remember asking the other people on the table to pass on their glacé cherry if they didn't want it. It was not until the mid-eighties that I realised cherries were not bright red and covered in a sticky syrup when in their natural form. The cherries have been replaced with raspberries in this recipe, and I find the rum adds a nice little kick to this longstanding national gem. Serves 6–8 (V)

50g butter, plus extra for greasing

50g soft light brown sugar

1 large can of pineapple rings in juice (about 7 rings), drained well

Splash of dark rum or a squeeze of lime (optional)

8 fresh or frozen raspberries

Sponge

125g butter, at room temperature

125g soft light brown sugar

Pinch of salt

2 eggs

Grated zest of ½ lemon

Seeds of ½ a vanilla pod or a few drops of vanilla extract

125g plain flour

1½ tsp baking powder

Good pinch of ground cinnamon

1 tbsp milk (optional)

Preheat the oven to 180°C (350°F), Gas Mark 4. Melt the butter in the frying pan over a high heat and immediately add the sugar. Stir continuously until dissolved and syrupy, then add the pineapple rings, placing one in the middle and the rest around the outside, and cook them for 3–4 minutes so they get a good colour on the bottom. Keep spooning the butter and sugar mixture over them, so the tops are coated and caramelised. Add the rum or lime juice, if using, and cook for a further minute until thick and syrupy. Take the pan off the heat, place a raspberry in the centre of each pineapple ring and set aside.

For the sponge, cream together the butter, sugar and salt in a medium bowl. Next, add the eggs, one at a time, beating hard between each addition. Add the lemon zest and vanilla and mix for a few seconds. Now stir in the flour, baking powder and cinnamon until well mixed. If the mixture seems a little stiff, add some milk to loosen it.

Carefully, from a low height, so as not to disturb the positioning of the pineapple rings, spoon the mixture in dollops around their tops. Gently spread the mixture out evenly using the back of the spoon until completely covered, being careful not to drag along any syrup that rises up.

▶

Caramelised pineapple, rum & vanilla upside-down cake (continued)

To serve

Mascarpone

Icing sugar or runny honey, to taste

Equipment

20cm diameter non-stick ovenproof frying pan

Bake on the middle shelf of the oven for 30–35 minutes, or until a skewer inserted into the centre of the cake comes out clean. The cake should be golden on top, feel springy to the touch and smell cooked. Leave to cool for a few minutes before very carefully turning the cake out onto a large plate. The best way to do this is to invert the plate on top of the pan and flip the pan and plate over at once, then remove the pan to reveal the upside-down cake.

Serve with a dollop of mascarpone sweetened with some icing sugar or honey.

Chewy white chocolate fudge cookies

After experimenting with flour, I found that adding some strong white bread flour to the cookie mixture makes the cookies extra chewy. If you do not have bread flour, just use 200g of plain flour – your cookies will still be delicious. Makes 6–12 cookies *(V)*

125g butter, at room temperature

225g soft light brown sugar

1 egg

150g plain flour, plus extra for dusting if necessary

50g strong white bread flour

1 tsp bicarbonate of soda

½ tsp baking powder

Pinch of salt

200g good-quality white chocolate, roughly chopped

Preheat the oven to 180°C (350°F), Gas Mark 4. Line a couple of large flat baking sheets with baking parchment.

Cream the butter and sugar together in a bowl until pale and smooth. Add the egg and beat in. Add the flours, bicarbonate of soda, baking powder and salt and gently stir together to give a smooth but slightly sticky mixture. Finally, fold in the white chocolate.

Divide the dough into six equal-sized pieces and roll each one into a ball. Use floured hands here if you feel the mixture is a little too sticky to handle. Flatten each ball between the palms of your hands so they are about 1cm thick and not quite a perfect round. If you want smaller ones, just make 12 balls instead.

Arrange three on each baking sheet, spaced a good 10cm apart, as they will spread during cooking. Bake in the oven for about 10–12 minutes until pale golden. They will still be quite soft to the touch, but remove them from the oven and leave to cool a little on the sheet for about 5 minutes. When slightly set, very carefully transfer them to a wire rack with a fish slice. These are so delicious still a little warm. Any leftover cookies can be stored in an airtight container for a couple of days.

Winter Swiss roll bowl cake

So easy, so stunning and no real cooking involved. The 'proper' name for this stunner is a Charlotte Royale, which originated in days of old. Serves 6–8 (V)

2 x jumbo chocolate Swiss rolls (not the chocolate-dipped ones) or 4 normal-sized ones

150ml alcohol of your choice, such as rum, sherry or limoncello (optional)

2–3 litres ice cream, chocolate or vanilla or both (not soft scoop), removed from the freezer so it is softened but still frozen (no warmer than -12°C)

Equipment

Medium glass bowl or pudding basin

Line the inside of the bowl with clingfilm so that it is overlapping the sides. Make sure that the clingfilm is touching the bowl and is 'fitted'. Cut the Swiss rolls into 1–1.5cm slices. Place one slice in the middle on the bowl in the base, then place another next to it. Continue until the whole inside of the bowl is covered. Squash the Swiss roll slightly together so that there are no gaps between the slices. When you reach the top of the bowl, just cut slices in half if a whole one does not fit.

Pour the alcohol of your choice, if using, into a small bowl, then use a pastry brush to dab the sponge with the alcohol. Spoon the ice cream into the bowl, squidging it down so that it is completely full. Now place the cake in the freezer and leave overnight or at least until the ice cream is completely firm.

Once the ice cream is firm, carefully remove the cake from the bowl using the clingfilm to help you. Ease it very gently out of the bowl with the clingfilm. If it is too hard to remove, let the bowl warm up a little with your hands by rubbing the bowl or by carefully running a flat blunt knife between the bowl and the clingfilm. When the cake is loose in the bowl and feels as if you could pull it out easily, let go of the clingfilm, then place a large serving plate on top of the bowl and turn the bowl upside down, so that the plate is the right way up. Carefully remove the bowl and peel off the clingfilm.

I LOVE this moment!!! Serve with some berries of your choice.

Graffiti cake

Another recipe that came to me at one in the morning. I was making a sugar syrup for toffee apples, and while rifling through the cupboards I found some food colouring, one in red and one in blue. As red is my favourite colour, it won the day and I dropped a few beads of the scarlet liquid into the mix and set about dunking the apples into the hot mixture. I swizzled it around and placed it on baking parchment and then did the same with a pear. Nice, I thought, but not very impressive, so I poured the hot mixture into a glass heatproof jug and lay a long piece of parchment on the work surface and started drizzling shapes onto it. At the time I had no idea what I was doing; fatigue had definitely set in. I glanced at a freshly iced sponge and then my mad food scientist mood kicked in. I lifted the band of now warm and hardening sugar and wrapped it around the cake – and so graffiti cake was born. Sometimes I can manage it in one piece, sometimes it snaps into several pieces, but I just stick that around the cake, either way, I rather like the way it looks! Serves 8 *(V)*

200g butter, softened, plus extra for greasing

200g soft light brown sugar

Seeds of ½ a vanilla pod or a couple of drops of vanilla extract

5 eggs, lightly beaten

200g self-raising flour

Sugar syrup

200g granulated sugar

200ml water

Buttercream

400g butter, softened

Seeds of ½ vanilla pod or a couple of drops of vanilla extract

800g icing sugar

Preheat the oven to 180°C (350°F), Gas Mark 4. Grease and line the bottoms of the pans with baking parchment and grease the sides with a smear of butter.

Cream the butter and sugar together in a bowl until soft and fluffy. Add the vanilla and one egg and beat the mixture like mad, then add another egg and beat it well. Add a couple of tablespoons of the flour, stir, then repeat, adding two more eggs, one by one, beating well between each addition. Add the rest of the flour and mix well to combine.

Divide the mixture between the two tins, smooth the mixture out a little with the spoon and bake on the middle shelf for 25–30 minutes, or until a skewer inserted into the centre of one of the cakes comes out clean. The cake will feel springy to the touch, will be golden brown and will smell cooked. Remove the cakes from the oven and leave to cool completely in the tins.

While the cakes are cooking, I like to make the sugar syrup. Put the sugar and water in a small pan over a low–medium heat and allow the sugar to dissolve, then turn up the heat and let the mixture boil for a couple of minutes. Take the pan off the heat and set aside.

▶

Graffiti cake
(continued)

Graffiti writing

250g granulated sugar

130ml water

130ml golden syrup or liquid glucose (liquid glucose can be bought from large supermarkets)

Enough drops of food colouring to your liking

Few drops of vanilla extract

Equipment

2 x 20cm round sandwich tins

Heavy-based medium pan with a long handle

Heatproof jug

As soon as the cakes come out of the oven, brush the tops liberally with the sugar syrup. If you have any syrup left over, store it in a sterilised jar for a week or so.

While the cakes are cooling, make the buttercream. Put the butter and vanilla in a large bowl and beat well with a wooden spoon until it begins to go light and creamy. Add the icing sugar, bit by bit, and beat together until combined and the mixture becomes lighter. Set aside.

To make icing the cake easier, put the cakes in the freezer for 20 minutes to get nice and hard. Put a cake board, if you have one, onto a plate and dollop some buttercream onto it, then take one of the cakes and place it on top of the buttercream. Spread the cake with buttercream and place the other cake on top. Now the fun bit: spread lots of the buttercream over the sides and top of the cake; spread it quite liberally at first, then smooth it out round the edges and over the top to give a neat first layer. Pop it into the fridge for the first layer to become hard (or use the freezer if you, like me, are a little impatient when it comes to cake). Once it is hard, remove it from the fridge and spread over another layer of buttercream. Try to get it smooth so the edges are really sharp.

Meanwhile, make the graffiti. Line a couple of baking trays with baking parchment. Have handy a jug, a cup of cold water with a spoon in and a cup of cold water with a pastry brush in.

Put the sugar into the heavy-based pan together with the water and golden syrup or liquid glucose over a medium heat. Swirl the mixture a little rather than stir it, otherwise the glucose can stick to the spoon. Once the sugar has dissolved, turn up the heat and let it boil away. If there is any sugar stuck to the side of the pan, brush it off with the wet pastry brush.

The sugar needs to be cooked for about 10–15 minutes, but check it every 5 minutes to see if it is ready. To check, take the teaspoon from the cup and dip it into the mixture, carefully scooping out some mixture, then put the spoon back into the cup and leave it there for a minute or so to cool down. Pick up the spoon and feel the sugar mixture on the end of the spoon. If it has disappeared, that shows that the mixture is in the very early stages of cooking. Let it boil again and test it using the same method; if the mixture is soft and a bit squidgy, it is still not ready. It will go through various stages until the hard crack stage – the sugar mixture will be rock hard on the end of the spoon when a bit is scooped out and plunged into the water and left there for a minute or two. The mixture in the pan will also start to go a very lightish brown colour.

Once the mixture reaches this stage, turn off the heat and add the colouring and flavouring. Stir as little as you can so it is just combined and then extremely carefully pour the sugar into the jug. Use oven gloves when handling the pan, as hot sugar can spit and burn you. Leave to cool for a minute or so, then drizzle a long band of graffiti squiggle shapes on the baking parchment. Use a hairdryer to keep the sugar syrup pliable if necessary. The graffiti can be as long as you like, but needs to be at least as high as your cake. Once you are satisfied you have enough bands (and it is good to have a few, as they do break), set the jug down and wait a few moments for the sugar to harden a little.

Remove the cake from the fridge. When the graffiti is firm but still pliable, carefully peel off the back of the baking parchment and stick the graffiti around the cake. If you have one long piece that can go round that's great, but small pieces done patchwork-style look good too. Once the sides of the cake are covered, you could arrange berries of your choice or chocolate shavings on top and serve.

‘Oat couture’ granola bars

I usually make a double batch of these bars and keep them in a tin in the fridge for a grab-and-go breakfast. Makes 8 bars *(V)*

125g butter

200g soft light brown sugar

250g porridge oats

75g pecans, toasted (fry them in a dry pan for 2 minutes, or until toasted) and roughly chopped

75g pumpkin seeds

75g raisins or another dried fruit (I also love dried cranberries)

100ml maple syrup

Equipment

20cm square baking tin

Preheat the oven to 180°C (350°F), Gas Mark 4. Line the base and sides of the tin with baking parchment.

Melt the butter in a large pan, add the sugar and simmer for 3–4 minutes, stirring, until the sugar dissolves and the mixture is bubbling. Take the pan off the heat and add the oats, pecans, pumpkin seeds, raisins and maple syrup. Stir everything together well to combine, then tip the mixture into the prepared tin. Squash the mixture down very hard with the back of a spoon. This bit is important so that the granola bars do not crumble when cut.

Bake in the oven for 30 minutes until firm and lightly golden on top. Take out of the oven and leave to cool in the tin.

When cool, carefully lift out with the help of the baking parchment and cut into eight bars. Store in an airtight container for up to four days.

Really very naughty chocky rocky road cake

When I make the batter for this cake, I feel like diving into the bowl. I know it's wrong but I still firmly believe that licking out the bowl is the best part of cooking. In fact, truthfully, it is one of the reasons I started baking in the first place. Makes 8 *(V)*

Oil, for oiling
125g butter, softened
175g caster sugar
50g mascarpone
5 eggs
165g self-raising flour
40g cocoa powder
1 tsp baking powder
½ tsp bicarbonate of soda
50g mini marshmallows, plus extra 10g to decorate
60g Maltesers, plus extra 20g to decorate
60g digestive biscuits or Rich Tea biscuits, crushed
60g white chocolate chips, plus extra 20g to decorate
2–3 tbsp milk or water (optional)

Icing

200g butter, softened
400g icing sugar
3 tbsp milk
100g dark chocolate (at least 70% cocoa solids), melted (see page 195)
60g crème fraîche

Equipment

2 x 20cm round sandwich cake tin

Preheat the oven to 180°C (350°F), Gas Mark 4. Oil the base of the tins with a little oil and line with greaseproof paper or baking parchment.

Cream the butter and sugar together in a large bowl until pale and fluffy. Add the mascarpone and stir through a little, then add two eggs and half the flour and beat well for a couple of minutes. Add the remaining eggs, the rest of the flour, the cocoa powder, baking powder and bicarbonate of soda and beat well for a couple of minutes until well combined. Fold in the marshmallows, Maltesers, crushed biscuits and chocolate chips. If the mixture looks a little stiff, add the milk or water and mix together.

Divide the cake mixture between the tins and bake in the oven for about 25–30 minutes, or until the cakes are cooked and spongy to the touch when pressed lightly with a finger.

Meanwhile, make the icing. Put the butter in a large bowl and beat very well, then add the icing sugar and milk and mix well. Gradually add the melted chocolate, stirring all the time, then fold in the crème fraîche until well combined. Set aside.

Once the cakes are ready, take the tins out the oven and leave to cool. When completely cool, take them out of the tins. Put a blob of the icing onto a serving plate and place the cake on top of the icing. Now spread some icing over the cake and place the other sponge on top. Spread the rest of the icing over the whole cake to cover. Scatter the extra marshmallows, malted chocolate balls and chocolate chips over the top and sides of the cake and serve.

Sweets, Jams & Other Good Stuff

Sweets, chutneys, popcorn and other tasty things are the subject of the final chapter in this book. As a child I used to know a lady who would make me some very fine chutney and give it to me in jars to take home. I would eat it with everything – from chips to bread to chopped-up vegetables. I never had myself down as someone who would become a chutney lady, sterilising jars and cutting up bits of fruit, but my apple, blackberry and cinnamon chutney tasted so good that I developed a bit of a habit and, just like in my youth, I have begun eating it with everything! The peppermint creams are another throwback to childhood and I challenge you to make them without eating the whole lot before you cut them out!

'The second day of a diet is
always easier than the first,
by the second day you are off it.'

Jackie Gleason

Apple, blackberry & cinnamon chutney

This wintry chutney is totally and utterly delicious and seems to go with absolutely everything. I made a pork belly roast recently and served it with this and they went really well together. I always have a few jars of chutney or some other preserve to hand, as they make great edible gifts. Makes about 1.3kg *(V)*

- 1kg Bramley apples, peeled, cored and cut into large chunks
- 300g onions, peeled and finely sliced (about 3 small–medium)
- 275g granulated sugar
- 150ml balsamic vinegar
- 2 tsp ground cinnamon
- 2 twists of black pepper
- 300g blackberries

The chutney needs to go into sterilised jars. The easiest way to do this is to put them in the dishwasher on the hottest cycle to wash and dry. Take them out when you are about ready to use them and don't touch any of the inside of the jars with your hands. Alternatively, put the jars in a very large pan of boiling water and boil for a couple of minutes before taking them out to dry on kitchen paper. You will also need to boil the equipment you use to take the jars out of the pan. At this stage, the jars can be popped into a low-temperature oven to dry. Make sure they are not cracked.

Put the apples, onions, sugar, balsamic vinegar, cinnamon and black pepper into a large pan over a medium heat and stir gently together. Slowly bring the mixture to the boil, then turn down the heat and leave the mixture to simmer for 45–55 minutes, stirring occasionally. The apples and onions should become lovely and soft, and the liquid should be thick and syrupy.

The blackberries need only a little while to cook, so add them at this point and cook for a further 10–12 minutes.

While the chutney is still warm, use a sterilised jug to fill the sterilised jars, then seal and store in a dark place. This chutney will keep for up to four months.

Bubble wrap sugar

A great thing to do with sugar, for spectacular decoration. It is tough to say how many this will serve, as it depends so much on the size which you make it. Give it a go if you can; it is great to see the bubble sugar, bubble! Serves 4–6 *(V)*

200g granulated sugar
80ml water
45g liquid glucose
2 tbsp vodka

Equipment

Baking tin, about the size of an A4 piece of paper

Scrunch up a piece of baking parchment about the same size as the baking tin, then unscrunch it, put it in the tin and brush it with vodka. Set aside.

Put the rest of the ingredients in a pan and boil until it just starts to turn light yellow. Don't stir the mixture but swirl it around if necessary. As soon as the mixture turns yellow, pour the sugar onto the paper and leave it until it is completely cold – this can take anything up to an hour (depending on the temperature of the room) – then gently peel off the baking parchment. Use to decorate desserts and cakes or serve crushed up with berries, with ice cream or with a shot of espresso.

Chocolate marshmallow brown sugar fudge

I love fudge, especially at the pick and mix, and whilst the cola bottles, lemon sherberts and jelly babies jostle for favour, the fudge wins every time. Having said that, though, the homemade ones are super good, and with no messing about with sugar thermometers you are pretty much guaranteed delicious-tasting creamy fudge with very little fuss. Makes 25 pieces *(V)*

Oil, for oiling
70g butter
300g soft light brown sugar
120g evaporated milk
220g small marshmallows
300g grated milk chocolate and 75g grated dark chocolate (at least 60% cocoa solids)

Equipment

20cm x 20cm square brownie tin

Oil the brownie tin, then line with baking parchment, making sure the baking parchment overlaps the sides so it is easy to take the fudge out once set.

Put the butter, sugar, milk and marshmallows in a pan over a low heat and melt gently. Once the sugar has dissolved, turn up the heat and let it boil for about 5–6 minutes. Take the pan off the heat and add the grated chocolate. Leave it for 1 minute, then stir the mixture together until everything is melted. Pour the mixture into the prepared tin and leave to set for a couple of hours. Once set, cut into 25 squares and serve.

Asian chilli jam

A fantastic 'jam' that is more like a chutney, this is good with fish, meat, charcuterie and cheeses and is a great little gift for family and friends too. I tie a ribbon around the top with a label and hand jars out as Christmas presents. Makes 1 small jam jar *(V)*

450g tomatoes, stems removed

2 cloves of garlic, peeled and roughly chopped

2 red chillies, deseeded and finely chopped

1cm piece of fresh ginger, peeled and grated or finely chopped

250g granulated sugar

60g balsamic vinegar

Salt and freshly ground black pepper

Equipment

Sterilised jar (see page 222)

Put all the ingredients in a blender and blitz, then add to a medium pan. Bring the mixture to the boil and boil for 25–30 minutes or so, stirring occasionally so it does not catch on the base of the pan. Cook until the mixture thickens and becomes syrupy. The thicker the mixture, the more likely it is to burn and catch. To test if the mixture is ready, remove a little of the jam with a teaspoon and leave to cool by the sink for 5 minutes or so; it should be quite thick and jamlike. If it is not ready, boil it for another 5 minutes or so.

Once the jam is cooked, take the pan off the heat and leave to cool for 20 minutes.

Now pour the jam into a sterilised jug and pour it into the sterilised jar. Place the lid on top without sealing and leave to cool before closing the lid tightly. Totally divine with cold meats.

Peanut butter truffles

These fine truffles require an overnight stay in the fridge or, at the very least, a good few hours. I make these time and time again as an after-dinner treat, or as a birthday gift for family and friends. If you fancy a change from peanut butter, flavour the truffles with stem ginger, mint essence or some coconut. Makes 15 x 25–30g balls *(V)*

120ml double cream

200g milk chocolate, plus extra 200g milk chocolate for the covering, broken into pieces

Knob of butter

5–6 tbsp crunchy peanut butter

Put the cream in a small pan and heat until it is almost boiling, then switch off the heat and add the chocolate and butter. Take the pan off the heat and leave to stand for about 6–8 minutes without stirring. After this time, very gently stir everything through until it is just combined. The mixture will become shiny and smooth.

Pour the mixture into a bowl and gently stir in the peanut butter. Leave to cool down a little, then pop it in the fridge for a few hours or overnight.

Once the mixture is firm, take the bowl out of the fridge. Line a large tray with baking parchment. Using a melon baller, 1 tablespoon measuring spoon or a couple of teaspoons, scoop up a spoonful of the chocolate mixture and quickly roll it into a ball. Place the ball on the baking parchment and continue with the rest of the chocolate mixture. If the balls are becoming too soft, put them back in the fridge for 15 minutes or so until firm. The chocolate is good enough to eat at this stage, but for a more finished look, I like to dip them in a little more chocolate.

Melt the remaining 200g milk chocolate, either in 20-second bursts in the microwave, stirring between each addition, or in a heatproof bowl set over a pan of boiled water, making sure that the bottom of the bowl is not touching the water and that the heat is off, otherwise the chocolate can seize and become grainy.

Once the chocolate is melted, it is time to dip the truffles. I find the easiest way to do this is to put a truffle on the end of a fork and dip it into the melted chocolate, dunking it under so it is covered, then allowing some of the excess to drip off. Pop the coated truffle back onto the lined tray and repeat with the rest of the truffles.

The chocolate truffles can be placed in little paper cases and boxed up as gifts, which are always a big hit.

Peppermint creams sugar rush

When I was younger, I was totally addicted to peppermint creams. I've had versions since which are covered in chocolate, but I love mine plain and simple. These sweets are great to make with kiddies, and can be ready in under 20 minutes.

Makes about 35 creams (V)

300g icing sugar, plus extra for dusting

125g condensed milk

¼ tsp peppermint extract or more, to taste

100g dark chocolate, broken into pieces

Equipment

Various cutters (optional), I used a 4cm round fluted cutter

Put the icing sugar, condensed milk and peppermint extract in a medium bowl and mix together to form a smooth soft dough.

Roll out the dough on a work surface dusted with icing sugar until it is just slightly thicker than a £1 coin. Cut out different shapes with various cutters, if you wish, re-rolling the mixture until it is used up. Keep any mixture you are not working on covered with clingfilm to avoid drying out.

Melt the chocolate in a heatproof bowl set over a pan of simmering water or put the chocolate in a plastic bowl and melt in the microwave at 30-second intervals, stirring in between each one. Dip some of the peppermint creams into the melted chocolate until they are half-covered, then leave to cool and set on a baking tray lined with baking parchment.

If you are storing the creams, pop them in an airtight container spaced apart, dusted with icing sugar and separated between layers of baking parchment to avoid them sticking together. They can be stored for two to three days.

The nutty brittle brigade

I know brittle has been done a thousand times before, but every time I used to go in to the newsagent, I would buy a pack. When I became a chef and learned how to make my own, there was no stopping me. I eat this as a snack on its own, crushed up on some yoghurt or dipped in some melted dark chocolate for a bit of indulgence. *(V)*

Sesame and vanilla brittle

150g granulated sugar
6–7 tbsp water
Few drops of vanilla extract
60g sesame seeds

Ginger pecan brittle

175g granulated sugar
5–6 tbsp water
165g whole pecans
1–2 tsp ground ginger

Macadamia and mint brittle

175g granulated sugar
5–6 tbsp water
130g macadamia nuts
Few drops of mint essence

Line a baking tray with baking parchment. Decide on the brittle you are going to make, then place the sugar, water and vanilla extract, if necessary, into a medium pan and heat very gently over a low–medium heat until the sugar has dissolved. Use a brush dipped in water to remove any bits of sugar stuck to the sides of the pan.

Once all the sugar is dissolved, turn up the heat and let it bubble furiously. If you have a gas hob, the flames should only be under the pan when boiling the sugar syrup, so make sure the flames do not 'lick' up the sides of the pan. If you find this is happening, switch to a smaller gas ring.

After about 6–8 minutes, the mixture will start to go from white to a light golden brown. If there any darker patches around the outer edges of the sugar syrup, just swirl the pan very carefully to mix. When the mixture turns from light golden brown to a honeycomb colour, add the nuts or seeds of your choice – and the ground ginger or mint, if making the one of the other flavoured brittles. Don't stir, but carefully swirl and tilt the pan around until all of the nuts or seeds are covered; try to do this all quite quickly. Use oven gloves when handling the pan, as hot sugar can spit and splutter and burn you.

Pour the mixture into the prepared tin and leave to harden. This should harden quite quickly, in about an hour or so as long as the kitchen is not too hot.

Once the brittle is hard, break it up into shards and serve.

To clean the pan, pour some water into it and put it on the hob to boil – any sugar syrup clinging to it should just disappear.

Winter spiced lemon curd with cinnamon & vanilla

I do love a good lemon curd. For something with a vaguely wintery feel, I wanted to try it with some oranges or mandarins. The resulting product was unsatisfactory, to say the least: the taste was good but the colour was a very murky dusky brown and was, I felt, not good enough for the book. So with a few adjustments, a winter spiced lemon curd was born with a touch of fragrant vanilla. Delicious on toast, in a meringue pie with a twist or poured into jars as an edible gift. Makes about 700g *(V)*

Grated zest and juice of 3 lemons

4 eggs, beaten and strained

350g caster sugar

100g unsalted butter

6 whole cloves

1 x 5cm piece cinnamon stick

2 star anise

¼ tsp vanilla extract

Equipment

Sterilised jars (see page 222)

Put all the ingredients into a heatproof bowl set over a pan of simmering water and stir until the sugar has dissolved. Continue cooking the curd for 20–30 minutes, or until thickened. Do not boil, otherwise you will get sweet scrambled egg. Strain into sterilised jars. Leave to cool before sealing tightly. Label and cover.

This curd will keep for 2–3 weeks in the fridge.

Flavoured butters

I like to keep these butters to hand in the freezer. Whenever I need some, I just slice a piece off and put the rest back in the freezer for another day. The tarragon butter is great stuffed under the skin of chicken before roasting, the garlic butter is delicious put on a piece of steak, and the Roquefort is so good, melted on top of a jacket potato or new potatoes. Makes about 200g garlic and parsley butter, about 300g Roquefort butter, and about 175g tarragon butter *(V)*

- 500g butter, softened
- 2 garlic cloves, peeled and mashed into a paste
- 3 tbsp finely chopped fresh parsley
- 150g Roquefort or Dolcelatte cheese, crumbled
- 3 tbsp chopped fresh tarragon
- Salt and freshly ground black pepper

Divide the butter evenly among three small bowls. Add the garlic and parsley to one, the Roquefort to the next and tarragon to the last bowl. Season each one well, going easy on the salt in the Roquefort one. Using a fork, mash each one to combine the flavourings evenly.

Spoon one of the butters into the centre of a square of clingfilm and wrap the clingfilm around the butter, squidging it into a sausage shape. Twist each end of the clingfilm to roll it up tightly and put it in the fridge or freezer until firm. Repeat with the remaining butters. The butters can be stored for up to 1 month.

Toffee caramel popcorn

I do like going to the movies, especially at the weekend after a hard week. I am thinking more and more now, though, that one of the main reasons I like going is so that I can munch on a whole bag of popcorn without a second thought. Some like sugared, others the salty kind, but for me the only way is toffee. Serves 2–4 *(V)*

- 1 tbsp sunflower oil
- 100g popcorn kernels
- 100g butter
- 100g soft light brown sugar
- 150g golden syrup or maple syrup
- Tiny pinch of salt

Heat the oil in a large pan over a medium–high heat. Add the popcorn kernels and give it a shake to coat in the oil. Pop the lid on and keep shaking it every 20 seconds or so. As soon as you hear the first pop, shake it a little more often. It will pop like mad for a bit and sound like a fireworks display and then start to slow down. You can turn the heat down a little at this point to prevent burning the popcorn. Keep shaking it every so often until only a few pops can be heard. Take it off the heat and leave to stand for a minute or so, then remove the lid and leave the popcorn to cool.

Meanwhile, put the butter, sugar, golden or maple syrup and the salt in a small pan over a low heat. Simmer for 2–3 minutes, stirring from time to time. Take the pan off the heat when it becomes syrupy and smooth. Use oven gloves when handling the pan, as hot sugar can spit and splutter and burn you.

Carefully pour half of the toffee caramel sauce over the popcorn, mix it around with a couple of wooden spoons so the popcorn is covered, then drizzle the remaining half in, again turning the popcorn around so that it is all covered.

Let the popcorn cool right down before eating, even though it is very tempting not to do so.

There are two very dirty pans to wash up. Just fill them both half-full with water and put them back on a low heat. Bring the water to the boil, and the bits should come off the bottom easily. Failing that, tip out the water, dry the pans with kitchen paper and tip table salt over the burnt-on bits – the next morning, the pans will wash clean easily.

Serve the popcorn with a glass of something fizzy and a great blockbuster movie. This is best eaten straightaway, but store any leftovers in an airtight container for a day or two.

Lollipops

These pretty little things are so easy to make. I am always extra careful when working with hot sugar syrup, of course, but the end result is quite stunning. If you make them during the warmer months and if your house is quite hot, they do have a tendency to wilt after a day or so, so if you can, make them on the day you need them or keep them in a cool place. Makes 14 (V)

250g granulated sugar

130ml water

130g golden syrup or liquid glucose (liquid glucose can be bought from large supermarkets)

Enough drops of food colouring to your liking

Few drops of strawberry/peppermint/lemon flavouring

Equipment

About 14 lollipop sticks or kebab sticks cut in half

Line a couple of baking trays with baking parchment. Have handy a jug, two cups of cold water and a spoon and pastry brush. Put the sugar into a heavy-based pan with the water and golden syrup or liquid glucose over a medium heat. Swirl the mixture a little rather than stir it, otherwise the golden syrup can stick to the spoon. Once the sugar has dissolved, turn up the heat to bring it to a boil and let it boil away. If there is any sugar stuck to the side of the pan, brush it off with the wet pastry brush.

The sugar needs to be cooked for about 10–15 minutes, but check it every 5 minutes to see if it is ready. To check, take the teaspoon in the cup and dip it into the mixture, then put the spoon back into the cup and leave it there for a minute or so to cool down. Pick up the spoon and feel the sugar mixture on the end of the spoon. If it has disappeared, the mixture is in the very early stages of cooking. Let it boil again and test it again; if the mixture is soft and a bit squidgy, it is still not ready. It will go through various stages until the hard crack stage, when the mixture will be rock hard when tested. The mixture in the pan will also start to go a lightish brown colour.

Turn off the heat and add the colouring and flavouring, stirring as little as you can so it is just combined. Extremely carefully, pour the sugar into the jug. Use oven gloves, as hot sugar can spit and burn you. Leave to cool for a minute or so, then pour circles onto the parchment, staggered and spaced apart, leaving enough room for the sticks. Lay a stick in each circle straightaway so it does not cool too quickly, then leave the lollipops to set. They will harden very quickly if the sugar syrup has been cooked correctly. Once the lollipos are hard, peel off gently and eat!

Wash the equipment in a really hot cycle in the dishwasher, or pop the pan back on the heat filled with water and boil it clean. Run the jug under the hot tap for a few moments, then put it through the dishwasher.

Index & Acknowledgements

Index

D

E

F

G

H

I

L

M

S

T

U

W

4·5 kg
10 lbs
TOWER

Acknowledgements

Life can be less than easy at times so it is always good to know you have a solid crew of people helping you along the way. There have been many ups and downs in the writing of this book and through it all, I have been lucky enough to have been supported along the way by a whole bevy of fabulous, inspiring and clever people.

So if you are my mate or the like and I have left you out, I am sorry really I am you know what a scatterbrain, scatterbox I can be sometimes, so I love you all the same.

Ok, here goes (unscrumples a rather ominous looking piece of A4 paper):

The stellar team at the BBC Janice Hadlow, Lisa Edwards, Alison Kirkham, Jane Bentham and Rebecca Ford. The programme makers who have had the job of having to stare at my face day after day, hour after hour, whilst filming and/or editing reams of film tape: the dazzling Rachel Purnell and Olivia Ball, the meticulous Xanna Stuart, Bridget Gregory and the musical-minded Nadia Agar-Smith, the very perceptive and hugely talented director Sir Ben Warwick (well not really a sir but it sounds good), Carl Green for his brilliant text communication and patience, Bella Sullivan, Adam Lloyd, Trudy Riches and Ben Dodds; for the great girls in the kitchen slaving away over a very very hot stove: Lisa Harrison, Michaela Bowles and Simone Shagam; Carlos Ferraz and Chase Aston for taming the unruly hair on my head, Fiona Jones, Allan Ford, Nick O'Dell, Steve Flatt, Orlando Stuart and Matt Ball, cameramen legends and David Fergueson for holding that sound thingy in the air for all that time without so much as a whisper of complaint. Sharon Hearne Smith and baby pearl, Carole Tonkinson, Helen Hawksfield and Annie Hudson, Myles New ace photographer. The stormers; Sarah Doukas, Simon Chambers, Paula Karaiskos, Lou Grima and Emily – missing you as always. Diana Wais, you are pure brilliance, Diana Colbert, Dave and Adam in Kensington.

My dear mum Audrey, dad Roger and step-mum Kate, My big bruv Jason and my little sis Francesca. Auntie Angela (our family's very own Delia), Victoria and James – we must get together more, Laurie Rose – you rock as always, Rodney – King of the hill and my kind of other brother, Tony Walker. Velma Rowe, Benny C, Pierre and Clare Koffman, Andrew Antonio. At Ella's Bakehouse Mark Fell, Amir Mazit, Manu Ogunleye and Patricia Chouderek and Rose Chorlton, January Ramirez, Jerine Spark, Nancy O'Connor. Professor David Foskett, Terry Mcusker, Janet Rowson, Andy Gatley, Faye and Ben Healey-Potter, my partners in crime at UWL and my super bright class mates at Uni (get on with those dissertations!).

The team at John Noel: John Noel, Jonny, Tiffany, Rachel and Polly. My patient, supportive and amazing partner Ged, my wonderful daughter Ella, Charlotte Mensah for those long days sorting out my barnet, Ewan Venters – food maestro of the UK, Maggie Draycott (dinner soon? We must!), Guy O'Keefe, Norie and Ted Lagmay, Catherine Loubet, Marco Pierre White, Marcel, Matthew Settle, Jackie O and Jackie Michaelsen, PJ Simmons and Satya.